MAKE IT, KEEP IT

Wealth strategies to practice medicine on your own terms

AMIR BALUCH, MD

Copyright 2016 Amir Baluch

All rights reserved. No part of this publication may be reproduced, distributed, or transmitted in any form or by any means, including photocopying, recording, or other electronic or mechanical methods, without the prior written permission of the publisher, except in the case of brief quotations embodied in critical reviews and certain other non-commercial uses permitted by copyright law. For permission requests, write to the publisher, at the address below.
Published in the United States by Financial Wellness MD, Dallas, Texas.

ISBN-10: 1530660599

ISBN-13: 978-1530660599

2200 Victory Ave #902,
Dallas, TX 75219, USA

FinancialWellnessMD.com

Ordering Information:

Quantity sales. Special discounts are available on quantity purchases by corporations, associations, and others. For details, contact the publisher at the address above. Orders by
U.S. trade bookstores and wholesalers. Please visit FinancialWellnessMD.com.

Printed in the United States of America First

Edition 2016

25 24 23 23 22 21 20 19 18 17   2 3 4 5 6 7 8 9 0

Book Design by Gail Seymour
Cover Design by Rob Williams, C5 Design

Cover Photography by Phaneendra Gudapati Chess Photograph by Fisher Photostudio

Dedicated to all my physician teachers who trained me to be where I am today, especially friend and anesthesia mentor Alan Kaye, MD, PhD.

And to all the physicians from whom I learned not just clinically but financially as well, I want to give something back that I believe can help everyone at least a little bit

Contents

Acknowledgements	xi
Preface	xiii

Part 1: Wealth and Wealth Preservation — 1

Introduction	3
The Make It, Keep It Approach	4
Wealth Preservation	6
Why Brilliant Professionals Need Financial Direction	8
Stress: An Organic Response to Money	11
Amir Says	14
A Professional's Observation of Financial Confusion	15
Stress in the Medical Profession	16
Financial Worries	16
The Pessimist and the Optimist	16
How to Be Optimistic about Your Finances	17
Step 1 – List Your Blessings	17
Step 2 – List Your Concerns	17
Step 3 – Learn and Understand Different Financial Vehicles	17
Step 4 – Consider Asking for Financial Help	18
Bottom Line	18
Amir Says	19

Part 2: Make It — 20

Financial Management	22
The "B" Word	23
Facing Up to Your Spending Habits	23
Assessing Your Finances	24
Making Your Budget Work	24
Increasing your income	24
Tightening your Belt	25

Restructuring your Debt	25

Coming to Grips With Debt — 26

List Your Income and Outgo – Assets and Debts	27
Identifying Bad Debts	28
Deciding Which Debts to Focus On:	29
Credit Cards, Compound Interest, And Minimum Repayments	30
Refinancing and Consolidating	30
Allocating Debt-Reduction-and-Investment Budget	31

Investing 101 — 32

The Three Types of Income	33
Understanding Investing	34
The Magic of Compound Interest and Leverage Combined 35 The Importance of Multiple Streams of Income vs. Diversification.	35

Principles of Investing — 37

Margin of Safety	38
Profit from Volatility	38
Know Yourself	38
Avoid Over-Diversification	39
Invest Long-Term	39
Use Leverage to Buy the Farm	40

Discipline — 41

Understanding Rates of Return — 47

Rule of 72	48
The Danger of Historical Averages	50

What You Know — 53

Financial Vehicles — 56

Savings Account	57
Certificate of Deposit	57
Annuities	57
Mutual Funds	58
Stocks	58
Life Insurance	58
Disability Insurance	58

Long-Term Care Insurance	59
Real Estate Investment	59
Alternative Assets	59
Amir Says	60
Real Estate	**61**
Vacancy Rates	62
New Construction vs. Existing Establishment Investment	63
Loan-To-Value Ratio (LTV)	64
Debt Coverage Ratio (DCR)	64
Capitalization Rate	65
Internal Rate of Return (IRR)	65
Cash flow	66
Alpha Risk	**68**
Long-Term Investment Guide	**72**
Focus on the Total Return on Your Investments	73
Don't Follow Popular Trends	74
Diversify and Stay Flexible	74
Calculated Risk Is Okay	75
Learn from Previously Failed Investments	75
Watch Your Investments Periodically	76
Conclusion	76
Part 3: Keep It	**78**
Coming to Grips with Taxes	**80**
How to Reduce Your Taxable Income	81
Make the Most of Tax Exemptions	81
Set up an LLC	82
Use Tax-Efficient Investment Vehicles	83
Why You Need a Self-Directed Roth IRA	**85**
Traditional IRA - 401K	86
Roth IRA	87
Self-Directed Roth IRAs	88
How to Self-Direct Your Roth IRA	89
Asset Protection: When Insurance Plays a Vital Role	**91**
Life Insurance	92

Term Insurance	92
Permanent Life Insurance	93
Disability Insurance	94
Long-Term Care Insurance	95
Mutual vs. Stock	96
Amir Says	96
Asset Protection	**97**
Foreign Asset Protection Trusts (FAPTs)	98
Domestic Asset Protection Trusts	98
Family Limited Partnerships	99
Pensions and Inheritance	99
Infinite Banking and the Rich Man's Roth IRA	**101**
Wealth Preservation and the Sudden Wealth Syndrome	**104**
Take a Timeout First	106
Assemble Your Team of Professionals	106
Beware of "The Posse"	106
Get a Comprehensive Financial Plan	107
Create a Wishlist	107
Get a Financial Education	107
Monitor Your Finances	107
Diversify Your Wealth	107
Create a Pension	108
Amir Says	108
Making the Most of Charity	**109**
Giving Makes You Happy	110
Giving is Good for Your Health	110
Giving Creates Community Ties	110
Donations Are Tax Deductible	111
Understanding the Deductible Value of Your Donations	111
You Cannot Deduct the Value of Your Time	111
Estate Planning During Your Lifetime	**112**
Make a Living Will	114
Create a Power of Attorney	115
Estate Planning for Your Legacy	**116**
What Is Estate Tax?	117
Why Can't I Just Give It All Away While I'm Alive?	117

Can't I Avoid Estate Tax by Setting up a Trust?	118
Do I Really Need to Make a Will?	119
Where Can I Get Help with Estate Planning?	120
Wealth Management and Family Offices	**121**
Types of Family Offices	122
Single-Family Offices	122
Multi-Family Offices	123
Wealth Management Firms	123
Private Banks	123
Private Banks vs Small Non-Bank Boutique Family Offices 124 How the Wealthy Allocate Their Assets	124
Leveraging Real Estate Crowdfunding	125
Private Equity	125
Amir Says	126

Part 4: Take Action	**128**
What Now?	130
Wealth Preservation Checklist	131
Join Me at Financial Wellness MD	138

Many thanks to my parents for believing in me, no matter what I wanted to do in life, and for always being positive.

Thanks also to Eric Mattingly for being a mentor to me and showing me the ins and outs of successful investing.

I thank my attorney Nate Dodson for keeping me out of trouble and being available anytime I had questions about asset protection, corporations, or real estate law.

Also, thanks to real estate mentors and team members Tony Ramji, Kenny Kok, Sami Ebrahim, and Mike Yarrito

Special thanks and gratitude to the guest authors who generously donated their time and talent to make this book possible:

David Drake, author of LIFEE Life Instructions for Entrepreneurs and Executives, and founder and chairman of LDJ Capital, who opened my eyes to the world of family offices;

Carlos Padial III, author of Conscious Millionaire, who provided an enlightening look at why too much too soon can be a bad thing;

Neil F. Neimark, MD, author of The Science of Positive Thinking, who helped me think about money in new ways;

Jocelyn Ibanez-Pantaleon, MD whose take on gratitude and optimism was perfectly timed; and Chad Armstrong, whose knowledge of insurance was seemingly inexhaustible.

Thank you all for your contributions.

Preface

Nothing is ever certain. No cash-flow stream can last forever. You never know what's going to happen in the future.

When I was applying to med school, I thought, "I'll just go to med school." I started applying and got a couple of interviews, and then sat home and waited for my acceptance letter. After everyone else got their letters, I found out **I didn't get in.** Everybody was surprised, including me.

It made me feel uncomfortable, thinking I'd been so sure I was going to get in. Then I started thinking about what to do if I wasn't going to go to medical school. I started looking for something else and took a series of short-term jobs. I was a personal trainer, a librarian, an EMT (emergency medical technician.) Meanwhile, I reapplied to med school and got in.

During that two-year hiatus, I started researching how other people were building wealth. I came across an interesting fact: **80 percent** of multi-millionaires made most of their wealth through investing in **real estate and alternative investments**. I was about 21, and I went off and bought some courses I saw in an infomercial in the early hours of the morning. It was so long ago, I either got the CD or the cassette version. I started out that way, just learning from whatever was marketed on TV and trying to get some mentors along the way.

Although not getting into med school the first time felt like a setback, it ended up being a good thing. It forced me to get a perspective on life and look at what everybody else was doing.

One doctor I knew about that time, for example, was an internal medicine doctor. He was doing really well, making well into seven figures, which is good for a primary care doctor. But the better you do; the more people want your money. So, he was trading in options, he invested in land in Las Vegas without even looking at it, invested into restaurants, and weird gimmicks. Just trusting the wrong people. Before he knew it, he was dangerously over-leveraged.

What he didn't realize was that when projects don't go well, you still owe people all the money you borrowed. He ended up getting all his wages garnished, so that he couldn't even operate his practice. He had to declare bankruptcy, and that was pretty much the end of his career. He lost his business, his home, his cars – everything. He, his wife and three kids had to move into a 1-bed apartment in a rough area of town, where the rent was $250 a month including water and electricity. Just watching someone who I thought was financially secure go from living in luxury to that apartment so fast was a major wake-up call for me.

By the way, the "clueless doctor" whose career I watched implode?

That was my father.

That's probably why I aimed this book at the medical community.

Afier that, I became apprehensive about finances. I went in the opposite direction, almost being overly cautious, and doing too much due diligence on any investments. I became a voracious reader on all topics relating to finance and investing and started acquiring mentors who had already made it. I learned from the streets that way.

Since they don't teach this stuff in medical school, I was determined to educate myself financially from the outset. I learned on the fly, from reading hundreds of books, by listening to experts and successful investors, by finding answers to every question. I had some small business failures in my early 20s and I also learned from that "school of hard knocks." I tried my hand at real estate fix-and-flips, but with no experience and no mentors, I made some expensive mistakes. Those were hard lessons and I've been smart enough not to repeat them. My experience and learning from my mentors have now allowed me to be a full-time contributor for Forbes magazine, to have made guest appearances on multiple podcasts, and see articles written about my investments in Dallas Business Journal.

Among financial professionals, the consensus is that doctors know little or nothing about money. They also tend to be altruistic, and a little too trusting. The issue with most medical professionals is that they just don't understand how money is made or lost in investments, ofien making them easy targets for scammers and get-rich-quick schemes.

I began to realize that with this prevalent lack of financial sophistication, most medical professionals are living a financially precarious lifestyle. Many have crippling debt and despite high incomes, have little or no monetary safety net. When this high income depends on showing up every single day, working long hours, and maintaining the ability to perform specific, highly skilled tasks, what happens if they become incapacitated, or burned out? How would they survive financially?

Make It, Keep It was a compilation of financial wisdom that I had learned from people over the last 15 years or so. The reason I wrote it was that I see so many physicians out there that are investing in things that don't make sense. They don't know how to do due diligence. They don't plan out their finances correctly. They have questions, and sometimes they don't even want to ask them because they don't want to admit their ignorance, and they end up learning by experience.

I've addressed a number of these issues myself and I also invited a few expert guest writers to provide introductions to more specific investment topics. I quickly realized that some subjects are just too vast to cover in such a short financial primer. FinancialWellnessMD.com includes a resource section to provide more in-depth explanations.

A detailed introduction to Financial Wellness MD is provided at the end of this book for those of you who are ready to embark on your real estate investment career.

It is my sincere hope that you will develop sound financial management skills and create a solid financial future for yourself and your family using this book and those to follow, as well as the resources available on our websites

Part 1: Wealth and Wealth Preservation

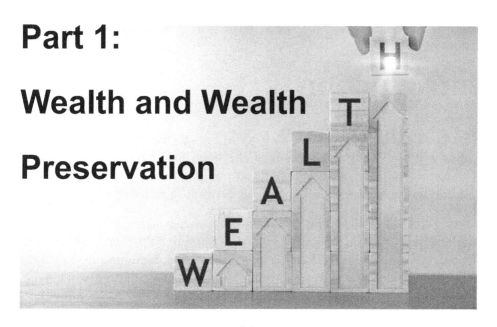

"When I was dealing with cancer, I was working on a book about finances. I realized that the same methodology that the doctors were using to cure me, you could use to cure your finances. Health and wealth are so linked, it's amazing."

Hill Harper

Introduction

This book and the supporting website at FinancialWellnessMD.com grew out of my increasing recognition of the need for financial education for physicians. As both an anesthesiologist and real estate investor, I'm often amazed and dismayed by my colleagues' attitudes toward money.

Getting through college and medical school is expensive, and the average student debt burden increases every year. In your third year of medical school with more than $160,000 in student loans, it's tempting to think, "I'm so far in the hole already, another $20 on a takeout order won't make any difference."

When you've sacrificed the first ten years of your adult life to qualify for your specialty, you're ten years behind your non-medical college pals, and have a mountain of debt, it's all too easy to blow that first huge paycheck. The problem is, it's also too easy to blow the second, third, and following checks, until you've created a lifestyle that consumes your salary and doesn't leave room to pay it off. Credit cards, car payments, country club fees, and the general cost of living mean you're a slave to your salary and live in constant fear of what would happen to you and your family if you were unable to perform your duties. Before you know it, you're approaching retirement with little to no savings, and you're faced with a choice; downsize and cut back or keep working long afier you planned to retire.

Too many medical professionals bury their heads in the sand at the mention of money, and then wonder why they're broke. Don't get me wrong – I'm a physician, too, so I get it. When you say, "I work long and hard, I deserve the good things in life," I agree. It's when these attitudes of fatalism and entitlement combine with the idea that doctors are inherently altruistic and not in it for reward, and that talking about money is taboo, that problems become entrenched.

I'm here to tell you if you want a secure retirement, you must stop burying your head. Take a long look at your finances and your attitude and make some changes.

You advise your patients to take responsibility for their own health. You tell them to eat well, avoid toxins, exercise, and maybe take supplements if they want to stay healthy for longer. If you want to be wealthy, you must take a similar approach. You must take responsibility for your own wealth. Budget, get out of bad debt, strategically get into good debt, invest, and make sure you have enough of the right types of insurance.

The *Make It, Keep It* Approach

This book is designed to be a financial primer. As such, it covers a broad range of subjects in brief. Each chapter addresses one common problem or question I'm ofien asked. Some are written by me, others are contributions from expert guest authors with my own comments at the end.

The book is presented in four major sections:

Part 1 introduces wealth preservation and discusses attitudes toward money.

Part 2 covers budgeting, debt reduction, financial vehicles, and the principles of investing.

Part 3 introduces methods to keep more of what you earn, including tax avoidance, pensions, insurances, asset protection and estate planning.

Part 4, the final section, encourages you to act and put into practice all you've learned.

Throughout this book, I use three fictional characters – Dr. Khan, Dr. Johnson, and Dr. Smith – to represent readers at three stages of their careers:

Dr. Khan is a 30-year-old resident physician. She earns $55,000 a year, rents an apartment with two roommates, and has $160,000 in student loans.

Dr. Johnson is a surgeon in his mid-forties. He earns $360,000 a year, has an $850,000 mortgage at 5.4%, is married, and has two young children he wants to put through college.

Dr. Smith is a family practitioner in his sixties, approaching retirement. He lives within his means and has a net worth of $2,000,000. He has no mortgage but made some investment mistakes in the past. He lost money in the stock market and has a few failed business investments in restaurants and physician-owned hospitals. This resulted in his retirement fund being far lower than what he hoped.

"How many millionaires do you know who have become wealthy by investing in savings accounts? I rest my case."

Robert G. Allen

Wealth Preservation

Before we dive into discussing the stages of wealth preservation, let me take a few minutes to define what I mean by that.

On the surface, it seems obvious. Wealth preservation is the process of ensuring you keep as much as you can of what you earn. As such, you might expect me to focus on minimizing taxes, creating pensions, and estate planning. Yet these subjects make up only a fraction of the subject matter.

So why have I included so much about the psychological aspects of wealth generation, money management, and investing in general? Because without the proper grounding in each of those, your chances of amassing wealth in the first place are diminished.

If you're in debt and that debt isn't tied to an asset earning a higher rate of return than the interest you're paying, you're bleeding wealth. Instead of being able to put your money to work for you, you're working for your creditors' benefit.

Wealth preservation must include investment strategies just to ensure your money doesn't stagnate and lose its spending power due to inflation. According to *Forbes* and Bureau of Labor statistics, monetary inflation is running at

3.9%[1]. So, if you leave your funds in any account earning less than that, you're bleeding wealth. From 1995 to 2005, consumer prices rose an average of nearly 3.5% every year. If you kept $1000 in cash during those years, by 2005, assuming no interest, the buying power of that money would have declined to about $700.

While you could work harder or longer hours to increase your income, if you're already working an 80-hour week you're limited in how much more you can take on. Instead, you must figure out how to use what you already must generate a future income that outpaces inflation, taxes, and associated fees.

To avoid excessive commissions and fees, you'll need to learn whom to trust, and what questions to ask to uncover the hidden charges. These can eat into the profits of many conventional investments such as stocks and shares, bonds, and CDs. You'll have to get comfortable with risk assessment and develop both a healthy skepticism and a willingness to do your own homework. For that, I've included several chapters on the principles and discipline of investing.

In financial terms, nothing is static. If you're not generating wealth, you're losing it. *Wealth preservation isn't just about keeping what you have, it's about growing it.*

---

[1] Forbes.com,. 2016. "Forbes Welcome".
http:/ www.forbes.com/sites/perianneboring/2014/02/03/if-you-want-to-know-the-real-rate-of-inflation-dont-bother-with-the-cpi/.

"Lack of financial instruction is the greatest deficiency of the medical establishment in our country."

Robert Doroghazi, author of
The Physician's Guide to Investing

Why Brilliant Professionals Need Financial Direction

"I spent more than a decade studying and gained multiple degrees. Nothing in my training prepared me to manage my income. Sure, I'm earning a good salary, but I feel like I'm ten years behind the people I went to college with. While they've been paying off their debts, buying houses and saving, I've just been racking up more debt. Now everyone assumes that because I'm a physician, I'm financially set. So why do I feel so insecure about my future?"

As a physician, brilliant professionals surround me daily – people who save lives, who enhance patients' quality of life, and who work long and hard to make the world a better place.

These people are highly intelligent, highly trained, and well-respected. They have the greatest confidence in their skills and practices, yet I hear the same complaint over and over again: "Why am I broke?" As a member of a rare breed – both physician and investor – my colleagues frequently approach me for advice. They know that because of my association with and learning from my mentors, I have both the experience and knowledge to weigh the good and bad of investments.

While I'm happy to give advice, I am frustrated by the lack of financial sophistication I so often encounter.

I'm not alone in my confusion.

Robert Doroghazi, author of *The Physician's Guide to Investing: A Practical Approach to Building Wealth,* says, "When it comes to money, many of our wonderful, dedicated physicians are utterly incompetent."

His woeful assessment is backed by research at University of California, in which interns scored just 40% on the Vanguard/*Money Magazine* Investor Literacy test. That score puts them on equal footing with the general population, but many financial experts see it as a sign of inadequate financial sophistication, particularly regarding investing.[2]

Doroghazi believes this lack of financial awareness is a failing of the medical educational system and finds it both reprehensible and endemic. Some level of financial

---

[2] *A Brief Educational Intervention in Personal Finance for Medical Residents* Gurpreet Dhaliwal, MD and Calvin L. Chou, MD, PhD Gen Intern Med. 2007 Mar; 22(3): 374–377. Published online 2007 Jan 17. doi: 10.1007/s11606-006-0078-z

education must be included in medical training programs, but the introduction of such training does little to help existing physicians. I urge my colleagues who come to me for advice to educate themselves. I say the same to you: If you do nothing else, read this book and the attendant resources. Do some of the exercises included in it and <u>act</u>.

With today's abundance of technology, the information anyone needs to research an investment is easily accessible. Yet so many health professionals, aware of the need to invest for the future, nonetheless allow fear of loss to paralyze them. Once you realize how to make the power of compound interest work for you instead of against you, you can understand the importance of starting NOW. Risk is inherent in any opportunity, but with a level head and sound planning, you can manage it. Procrastination and inaction have a <u>zero</u> rate of return.

Upcoming chapters explain the difference between income and net worth; assets and liabilities; and spending vs. investing. I also introduce different types of income, the importance of generating multiple streams of revenue, and the truth about diversification.

Each chapter includes a resource list with additional suggested reading materials and a link to FinancialWellnessMD.com so you always have access to the most current information. Take advantage of these and you can approach investing with confidence.

"Do not spoil what you have by desiring what you have not; remember that what you now have was once among the things you only hoped for."

Epicurus, Greek philosopher, 341-270 BC

Stress: An Organic Response to Money

Neil F. Neimark, MD

Author, *The Science of Positive Thinking*Board Certified, Family Practice
Fellow of The American Institute of Stress

http://www.neilmd.com

"I became a doctor because I wanted to heal people, but it's a physically, mentally, and emotionally demanding occupation. It doesn't leave me with much time or energy for anything else. I earn good money but dealing with it stresses me out even more. How can I make handling my finances less daunting?"

Money is perhaps one of the most challenging and misunderstood concepts in modern-day life. We work hard for money. We worry about not having enough. No matter how much we acquire, we want more. Then the more we get, the more we worry about losing what we have. Money, the endless striving for it, the unquenchable thirst for more, and the fear of losing it creates a remarkable amount of stress.

Unrealistic expectations about money abound. We are exposed daily to stories of new startups generating millions of dollars, online gurus earning hundreds of thousands a month, and business ventures reaping income at astonishing rates. If we buy into these stories, we create unrealistic expectations about money that only add to our stress.

Though astounding financial successes do occur, most of them result from hard work, resilience, perseverance, and a series of prior failures or learning experiences. When we focus on success and financial abundance without regard for the massive effort expended to achieve it, we set ourselves up for great disappointment – chasing a mythical pot of gold at the end of some imaginary rainbow. As the great American comedian Eddie Cantors said, "It takes twenty years to make an overnight success."

All that doesn't mean we shouldn't put forth the years of study, struggle, and determination necessary to become an "overnight" success. Nor does it mean that achieving success is not a worthy goal. It's part of our destiny as human beings to also be human <u>doings</u> — to make our best effort to improve our character and realize our full potential. It is what gives most of us meaning and purpose to our lives.

Author and personal growth expert Jim Rohn says,

> "The greatest reward in becoming a millionaire is not the amount of money that you earn. It is the kind of person that you have to become."

Two of my favorite financial philosophies come from the *Talmud* — the second holiest book in Judaism. Though more than 2000 years old, it contains timeless wisdom that can help us live better lives today.

The first principle is: "The more possessions, the more worry."

The more money we have, the more we worry about caring for it, investing it, and protecting it from loss. Not having enough money creates worry as well. The key becomes finding the balance between extracting the most happiness from our current situation, while at the same time working to achieve and acquire more.

We must be wise in our wanting, or happiness will elude us. The cycle goes something like this:

- We crave money, confident it will bring us happiness and fulfillment.
- We get more money.

- We realize it doesn't bring us the satisfaction we expected.

The solution is in the next passage from the *Talmud*, in the form of a question: "Who is rich?"

The answer: "One who is content with what they have."

Without the ability to be grateful and feel a measure of satisfaction with what we already have, we will forever chase that rainbow, hoping it brings us contentment.

Best-selling author of *The Power of Now*, Eckhart Tolle, says, "Stress is caused by being 'here' but wanting to be 'there.'" Thus, the dilemma. How do we manage the gap? If we are content with where we are, we may never strive to improve ourselves. That means we might never grow to our full potential. A certain amount of stress is good and motivates us to grow. If the gap is too big, we are subject to a counterproductive and dangerous level of stress.

Harvard psychologist Daniel Gilbert teaches that humans are poor at predicting their future happiness. Virtually everyone (myself included) falls prey to the belief that more money will make us happy. True, more money may reduce stress if we don't have enough, but it can create new stress. Even a brief look at the fate of lottery winners tells us how true this is. The majority are either more insolvent, more miserable, or more depressed after winning than they were before.

A commonly held spiritual principle teaches that money is a magnifier. If you are already happy, more money can make you happier. If you are miserable and unhappy, it can magnify your misery.

Choose to find contentment where you are. Learn to be happy, satisfied, and grateful first. Then, no matter what level of financial success you achieve, it magnifies the joy and happiness you already have. This is the path to true wealth, both spiritual and financial. An added benefit—no one can rob you, rip you off, or scam you out of your happiness as they might your money. Investments in financial matters can be risky; whereas investments in attitude are risk-free and pay hefty dividends for a lifetime.

> There is a wonderful story about the great Sufi poet Nasrudin running down the street, chasing after something important.
>
> A friend, witnessing his chase, asks Nasrudin, "Where are you running?"
>
> "Can't you see? I'm chasing after my good fortune!" Nasrudin replies.
>
> "But Nasrudin, what if your good fortune is behind you, and it's trying to catch up to you?" his friend says.
>
> The moral of the story in modern psychological lingo: Be mindful of the moment and savor all the good in your life right now.

Amir Says

Neil's wise words serve as a reminder to us all of the importance of keeping money in perspective. Although this book's focus is wealth acquisition and preservation, I agree that the pursuit of wealth should never put your health and happiness at risk.

Nor should you assume that dollars earned equates to profit. When you hear talk of startups, gurus, and businesses making millions, it helps to remember the costs involved in generating them, and the associated risk of failure. If you find yourself envious of another's success, try reading up on some of the most spectacular business and financial implosions in history. For every Sony, there's a Betamax; for every Apple, a Commodore.

When it comes to creating wealth, keeping a level head, educating yourself, and investing based on sound information most often outperforms rushed decisions.

Never let the fear of missing an opportunity blind you. You'll be happier, healthier, and wealthier in the long run.

"Investing in what is comfortable is rarely profitable."

Robert Arnott

A Professional's Observation of Financial Confusion

Jocelyn Ibanez-Pantaleon, MD

Medical Writer and Fitness Blogger
Owner/Resident Physician, Pantaleon Polyclinic

http://globalmedicalwriting.com

"I receive multiple offers to invest in various opportunities. I don't know how to identify a good investment, so I end up doing nothing, then waiting for the 'right' opportunity to come along. How can I overcome this paralysis of confusion?"

Feeling confused and overwhelmed can lead to procrastination, a natural response to a lack of knowledge and experience in any field. Knowing you need to invest to preserve your wealth and secure your future, but not knowing how to make good financial decisions generates stress. While stress is healthy and can push you to improve your performance, behavior, and cognitive functions, having a negative attitude without relief can also lead to distress, depression, and other health problems.

Stress in the Medical Profession

I know firsthand being a doctor is a stressful profession. I've heard the same complaints from lawyers, commercial pilots, corporate executives and others. Repeated stress throws your nervous system into a "fight or flight" response, a phenomenon also known as burnout. When burnout sets in, most people, including doctors, can only see potential harm in their decisions, not the good outcome of their choices.

Financial Worries

Although many consider the medical profession a one-way ticket to riches, many medical students grow disillusioned once they start practicing. Physicians earn an average annual six-figure income, but these headline figures only tell part of the story. For a regular Joe entering medical school, this means shouldering an average medical school debt of $166,750 that takes 30 years to repay at about 7.5%.

Having a hard time making their financial ends meet, many doctors worry about their future and their kids' futures, their inability to keep up with the lifestyle they expect from their profession and having enough money to spend once they reach their senior years. As an added insult, many witness a decline in their earnings as their annual compensation gradually falls. This can lead to a chronic fear of impending financial doom.

The Pessimist and the Optimist

Worrying about money leads to stress and encourages a pessimistic outlook. Pessimism born of fear and ignorance grows into skepticism and closes the doors for creativity and possibility. Focusing on your financial worries causes you to fear what your future holds, and you create a self-fulfilling prophecy. By adopting a more positive outlook, your concern can instead trigger inspiration to save money or even "create" more money.

How to Be Optimistic about Your Finances

If you're stuck in a pessimistic spiral of stress and worry, adopting an optimistic outlook can be tough. Here are simple steps you can take to shift your mindset.

Step 1 – List Your Blessings

Gratitude is the science of counting your blessings. The more blessings you count, the greater happiness, hopefulness, and energy you feel. You can always use this energy to produce more money. Pessimism reaps depression, loneliness, anxiety, and neuroticism. Gratitude helps you cope better with stress, encourage you to create more positive behaviors, and strengthen and nurture your relationship with your spouse, kids, and loved ones.

When was the last time you listed all the things you are grateful for? Thanked your loved ones for being with you when you need them the most? Don't just think about your blessings, write them down, and act on your gratitude.

Step 2 – List Your Concerns

Write down all the money-related concerns you have in your head. The simple act of recording them frees up your mind from remembering them. Now, beside each concern, list all the possible options you can think of – no matter how unrealistic they may sound — to overcome them.

Step 3 – Learn and Understand Different Financial Vehicles

Most doctors perform well when managing their patients' health. Med school taught them the art and the skill of healing every part of the human anatomy. Yet this same school never educated them about how to spend wisely and keep their pockets full even afier retirement.

Being optimistic means accepting the challenge of conquering financial difficulties; and conquering financial difficulties means you need to have the proper knowledge to manage your earnings. Only with knowledge can you escape this fee-for-service world and invest your savings for a stable retirement plan.

Step 4 – Consider Asking for Financial Help

If you are not experienced, or have a poor record of handling your assets, you might consider asking the help of an experienced financial planner. A financial planner can help you determine the best asset allocation for your present lifestyle. You can also ask for a retirement lifestyle forecast and determine the best estate planning strategy for your situation.

Bottom Line

Maintaining a positive attitude is imperative to increase our capacity for health, peace of mind, and happiness. Having a positive attitude is also an important component of achieving and maintaining wealth. Asking your partner for an opinion and finding the right financial advisers and investment experts are not signs of weakness. If you have colleagues with experience, they can offer advice to help you decide. It takes a positive attitude to ask questions and act on the answers to improve your present financial situation, your future, and the future of those close to your heart.

Amir Says

I appreciate Jocelyn's direct approach. Just as you wouldn't hesitate to ask for a second or third medical opinion, knowing when to take financial advice is a sign of strength, not an admission of weakness. I hope this honesty opens the door to communication among us to discuss finances and investments, for as Benjamin Franklin said, "An investment in knowledge pays the best interest."

Jocelyn also touched on the need to escape the fee-for-service, or hours-for-dollars mentality. The average medical professional may be highly paid, but theirs is a relatively short career, preceded by many years of debt-inducing training. Even the highest paid surgeon enters practice on a salaried basis, with perhaps 30-35 years to save and invest for retirement, and an earnings peak afier as few as five years.[3] Whether it be from reduced reimbursements from insurance companies, being bought out by corporations and then salaried for less than their previous income, or competition from new physicians, many doctors are alarmed to find their income quickly plateaus, and even declines throughout their medical practice. All of this reinforces the need to look beyond medicine for supplemental income and investments.

When soliciting financial advice, consider the restraints your advisor works under and the basis on which advice is offered. An advisor working on a commission basis will only recommend products they can earn commission on, such as stocks, bonds, and mutual funds, and may only be required to advise you based on suitability standards. A fiduciary advisor, operating on a fee basis (whether hourly

---

[3] Pezzi, Kevin. 2016. "A Novel Look At Physician Income: Why A Medical Career Is The Wrong Career If Money Is One Of Your Primary Motives". Er-Doctor.Com.
http://www.er-doctor.com/doctor_income.html.

or performance-related) is required to base advice on your best interest, rather than his own potential income.[4]

Part 2: Make It

Know what you own, and know why you own it."

Peter Lynch

Financial Management

"I spent so long training and work so hard for the money I make. I want to enjoy it while I can. At the same time, I know I need to put something away for my retirement. But the pressure to maintain a certain lifestyle is intense. How do I gain control of my finances to allow me to invest?"

One of the hardest things to which newly qualified physicians must adapt upon completion of residency is the sudden and dramatic increase in income. Whether you scrimped and saved your way through medical school or racked up serious student loans, when you start to see the rewards for all your effort, it's tough to resist the temptation to spend, spend, spend.

Spending, however, does nothing to increase your net worth. If you want to be comfortable in retirement, and less dependent on your salary throughout your working life, converting a high income into high net worth is the name of the game. You do this by investing in assets and building your creditworthiness, while also paying down debts, reducing unnecessary spending, and minimizing liabilities.

The "B" Word

Now how do you apply all of this to your personal circumstances?

First – Know what you own and what you owe.

Second – Create and work within a budget that allows you to live within your means and increase your net worth over time.

I'm not going to pretend that budgeting is fun. It's tedious. It involves facing your true spending habits instead of ignoring them. If you're overspending, it means accepting you may have to change your attitude, and that can be a painful process. If you want to get to grips with your finances, though, budgeting isn't just important, it's imperative.

There are three basic steps to budgeting: collect your bills, statements, and receipts, and enter them in your budget to see what you're really spending; assess your finances; and troubleshoot to make your budget work.

Facing Up to Your Spending Habits

If you've never made out a budget before, this can be a real wakeup call. I'll help you get started:

Collect all your bank statements, credit agreements and other financial papers, and make two columns on a sheet of paper. On one side, list all your sources of income, from monthly salary to income from second jobs, consulting work, book royalties, interest from cash accounts, dividends from stocks and bonds, rental income, and anything else you receive regularly. List your net income afier taxes and other deductions – the actual amount you receive.

In the other column, list all your outgoing expenses. Monthly payments such as mortgage or rental payments, loan payments, insurance premiums and service charges are all easy to list, as you'll find them on your bank or credit card statements. Remember to add in discretionary, occasional and cash spending, too.

Account for birthdays, anniversaries, and seasonal gifis; vacations, travel, and entertainment; groceries, clothing, and impulse buys. You may find it easier to look over the past three months, estimate your annual spending, and allocate 1/12th to a monthly budget. I recommend creating a 12-month budget and allocating spending when it occurs, so you can keep track of those expensive months, and then avoid spending too much in the months preceding them. You can download an annual budget worksheet at FinancialWellnessMD.com in the support materials for this book.

Assessing Your Finances

Once you have your income and expense totals, it's a simple matter to deduct spending from income to see whether you are living within your means or overspending. If you use the annual budget planner in the

FinancialWellnessMD.com resources, identify upcoming months where finances may be tight and plan for them.

Making Your Budget Work

If your budget shows you earn more than you spend, congratulations! You can now see how much you have available to invest monthly. Start by setting up a savings account and transferring the excess amount monthly. That way, you ensure your spending doesn't creep up and engulf your disposable income. The best idea is to set up a scheduled transfer at the beginning of the month, as soon as you receive your salary. If you wait until the end of the month to make the transfer, chances are you'll spend more, leaving you less to invest.

If your budget shows your expenses exceed your income, you have three options: increase your income; reduce your discretionary spending; or restructure and manage your debts.

Increasing your income

Since this book aims to teach you how to increase your unearned income and portfolio income rather than increasing your earned income, I won't get into too much detail about that option just yet. We discuss it more in later chapters on the basics of investing. However, since these options require a budget balanced enough to free up at least a minimum for investment, consider consulting work or other side gigs, if your main employment allows moonlighting.

If you can't work more hours, sell some of your unwanted possessions. Hold a garage sale. Get rid of clutter and unused gadgets. You don't need them, and you might be surprised how much more you enjoy your home when it contains only the things you need.

Tightening your Belt

Consider your discretionary spending and where you can make cuts. Yes, you earn good money; and yes, you worked hard to get where you are. You deserve every penny. Don't let anyone tell you otherwise.

Just don't let the pressure to live up to a lifestyle dictate your spending. If you don't use the gym, don't keep paying for membership. Drive the car you can afford, not the one you think projects the right image. Eat in, rather than dining out, and brown bag your lunch for a few months. Check your cellphone usage and pay for the plan with the lowest call and data allowances that fits your needs. Evaluate every outgoing monthly cost and challenge yourself to cut as much as you can.

I drive a used car, rather than pay a few thousand dollars for the privilege of being the first to drive it off the lot. I've even been known to get my hair cut by trainees. I challenge myself every month to find new ways to spend less. Turn it into a game and see how much you can save each month by altering your spending habits.

Restructuring your Debt

If servicing your debts affects your ability to live from month-to-month, you need to act. Dealing with debt is easy to talk about, but often tougher to do. Acknowledging you have a debt problem takes courage, especially when you're a high earner. In the next chapter, we look at debt in more detail.

*"Today, there are three kinds of people:
the haves; the have-nots; and the
have-not-paid-for-what-they-haves."*

Earl Wilson

Coming to Grips with Debt

I know I need to start investing to build a portfolio, but I get conflicting advice about investing while in debt. Some say I should start investing even a small amount right away, while others say I should pay off my debts first. Who is right, and how can I reduce my debt burden sooner?

Confusion over the dilemma of investing while still in debt is a common cause of procrastination. Deciding whether to start your investment career, or focus on paying down debt, is to some extent a personal issue, but there are a few simple guidelines you can follow to help you decide your best course of action.

List Your Income and Outgo – Assets and Debts

If you did the budgeting exercise in the last chapter, you already listed your income and outgo. If not, make one before you continue with this exercise. Now it's time to create another list – of your assets and debts/liabilities. You can make this list on a sheet of paper, or you can download a spreadsheet from the resources section of FinancialWellnessMD.com.

For each asset, list it with a brief description, current value, purchase price, where it is held, and any associated income.

Remember, an asset isn't just something you own. It's something you own that provides a future economic benefit, i.e., it has intrinsic sales value (which is likely to increase in line with or above inflation), or it generates an income.

A liability represents a future financial obligation. Debts are the most obvious liability, but some possessions you consider assets may be liabilities. Your own home, despite its sale value, is usually a liability. Vehicles that have depreciated in value below the purchase price and have associated loans become liabilities. Club memberships, cellphone subscriptions, and other service contracts are liabilities. In recognition of the non-economic lifestyle benefits these liabilities offer, they are ofien referred to as non-financial assets.

If owning something produces a net gain, it's an asset; if it costs you money to maintain, it's a liability. The difference between the value of your assets and liabilities is your equity, or net worth. That's an oversimplification, but at this stage simple is good. It makes differentiating between spending and investing even easier. Money you use to buy an income-generating asset, be it capital, equity, or equipment or qualifications that increase your earnings potential, is investing. Everything else is spending.

Now list your debts, recording the name, to whom you are liable, balance outstanding, frequency and amount of scheduled payments. Record any early repayment or exit penalties, as well as interest rates.

When you have added everything to the list, match up liabilities to their underlying assets, where applicable. It helps you identify assets that cost you more to maintain than you realize, and highlights 'lifestyle' debts that have no underlying assets.

Your list might look something like this:

Assets	Purchase Price	Market Value	Held With	Income
1234 Home St	600,000	800,000	Chase Bank	0
234 Rental St	150,000	180,000	Bank of America	$200/month

Liability	Held With	Balance	Payment	Interest/Exit Penalty
2015 Mercedes SL 55	Dallas Credit Union	65,000	1200/month	2.99%
Student Loan	Physician Loans	170,000	700/month	3.25%

Identifying Bad Debts

Used well, debt is an excellent way to build your net worth. It's also a way to sabotage your finances. While there are many ways of defining the difference between good and bad debt, good debt allows you to leverage your finances to purchase income-producing assets or assets with the potential for capital gain.

To be classified as a good debt, the outstanding amount on the loan must be less than the value of the asset, with an interest rate below the income production or capital appreciation rate. Provided it's cheaper to mortgage your home than rent similar property in the same location, the first mortgage on your own home is also considered good debt, since it's likely to appreciate.

At the other end of the scale, bad debts that are easy to identify include high interest loans with an interest rate greater than 10%, loans against depreciable assets such as auto loans, and loans against consumable or durable goods such as store card and credit card balances.

Between these two extremes are various nuanced levels of debt, which are considered good or bad depending on your circumstances. A second mortgage or home equity loan used to fund home improvements that increase the value of the property, for example, is a good debt. The same loan used to pay for vacations and other lifestyle choices is a bad debt. However, used to consolidate existing bad debt into a single lower-cost repayment – provided you don't then use your newfound disposable income to buy more debt – although not increasing the underlying value of the asset, may still be considered good debt.

Once you have identified bad debt, the first step to recovering your finances is to stop adding to them. Don't spend anything on a credit card you can't afford to pay off in full before the repayment date. Cut up store cards and consider your credit card for emergencies only. If you must spend on it, revisit your budget, and find a way to reduce your spending over the coming months to pay it off.

Deciding Which Debts to Focus On:

Work through your list of loans. Either grab three different colored highlighters, or make marks in the margins, such as #, * and %.

- Highlight any debts with interest rates over 10% with one color or symbol.
- Highlight debts not tied to assets with a different color or symbol.
- Highlight loans tied to depreciable assets with a third color or symbol.

Your first targets are high interest loans either not tied to assets or tied to depreciable assets. These are followed by loans with no underlying assets and finally, loans with depreciable assets.

Credit Cards, Compound Interest, And Minimum Repayments

We talk more in later chapters about compound interest in terms of investing, but if you carry debt, it's important to understand how compound interest can work against you.

Say you have a credit card balance of $5,000, at 18% annual interest. The minimum payment amount may be as low as 1% plus interest per month, with a starting minimum repayment of $120. As your debit balance reduces, the minimum repayment is reduced.

If you repaid the reducing minimum each month and never spent on the card again, it would take you 31 years and eight months to clear the balance. It would cost you $6,760 in interest, for a total cost of $11,760.

If, instead, you repaid the same $120 each month, you would repay the debt in five years and three months, with interest of $2,521, and a total cost of $7,521. Increase your monthly payment to $150, and you would clear the debt in three years and ten months, and repay only $6,761 in total, about the same as you would pay in interest alone if you made only minimum repayments.

Refinancing and Consolidating

Check the exit or early repayment penalties for these loans and consider moving the balance to an alternative product with a lower interest rate. Be sure to factor any arrangement fees into your calculations.

If you have multiple high-interest loans, consider refinancing and/or consolidating them into a single loan with a lower monthly repayment and lower interest rate. If, however, you have several smaller, high-interest loans nearing the end of their repayment terms, consolidation can end up costing you more, even at the lower interest rate, because you extend the repayment term. Before taking this option, always compare the length of the consolidation loan and its overall cost against the cost of paying down several smaller existing loans.

Allocating Debt-Reduction-and-Investment Budget

Before you refinance, calculate the total you pay each month in loan repayments and designate that as your debt-reduction-and-investment budget. Once you move high-interest balances to lower interest options, start paying that difference into a savings account.

If you have remaining bad debts, concentrate on paying off the highest interest debt first. Channel the difference between your minimum payments and your budget into paying off the highest interest loan first. Once that debt is repaid, start making regular overpayments on the next-highest interest rate loan until that, too, is repaid. Continue using the monthly surplus gained from repaid loans to pay off those remaining until all your bad debts are repaid. This is known as the "snowball method."

When your debts are cleared, you then use the allocated funds to start investing.

To see whether it's better for your financial health to consolidate or "snowball" your debts, visit the resources section of FinancialWellnessMD.com and access debt consolidation and snowball calculators.

"Compound interest is the eighth wonder of the world. He who understands it, earns it ... he who doesn't ... pays it."

Albert Einstein

Investing 101

I've put my basic finances in order, I'm spending less and saving more, but the rate of return on my savings accounts is barely keeping up with inflation once tax is deducted. I have a safety net, but I want to put some of my money to work to build a real nest egg for my retirement. What's the best way to get started?

It's great that you're thinking in terms of putting your money to work, rather than working harder yourself. Understanding the need to focus on passive and portfolio incomes to build your net worth is the first – and maybe most important – step to becoming an investor. It also pays to have a clear understanding of what investing is and isn't; the magic of compound interest and leverage; and the difference between multiple streams of income and diversification. Then, although there is no one 'right' investment strategy or approach, you can see that rental real estate syndication is an ideal starting point.

The Three Types of Income

As I already mentioned, there are three types of income: earned income, portfolio income, and passive income. Imagine you have three buckets, labeled Earned, Portfolio, and Passive Income.

Earned, or active income is what you receive by trading dollars for time or effort. It's your salary, or business income where you are active in the business, consulting or appearance fees, and anything else whereby if you stop doing, the money stops coming. Since there are limited hours available to generate this type of income, even the highest salary has an inbuilt earnings cap. If you want to add money to the bucket labeled Earned you must physically go and get it.

Portfolio income comes from the sale of owned assets and is often referred to as capital gains. Portfolio assets can be real estate, antiques, art, collectibles, or paper assets such as stocks and bonds. When you buy or acquire assets, they sit on a shelf above the bucket and only go into the bucket when you sell them for a profit.

Unearned, or passive income is generated by assets you own or have created. These include royalties on intellectual property rights; rental income from real estate; profits from a business where you are not active; and interest and dividends from stocks, bonds, and other paper assets. The magic of passive income is that your assets collect the money for you.

Some assets, such as dividend-paying stocks and rental properties, generate both passive income while you own the assets, as well as unearned income at their disposal.

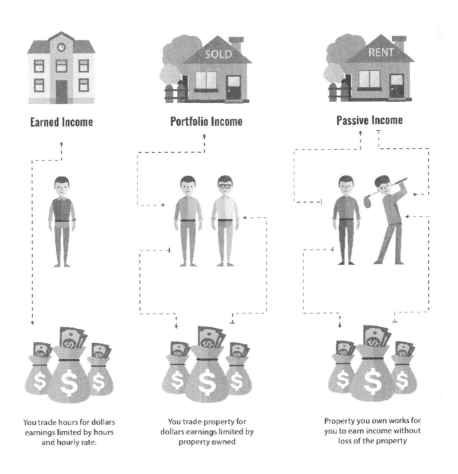

Understanding Investing

It's vital at this point to understand the long-term nature of investing. One definition of investing is putting your money to work with the expectation of additional income or increased asset value over time. It's not speculating – the buying and selling of assets quickly in hopes of high returns – which has more in common with gambling. At base, a gambler takes on the greatest risk, betting on an outcome that may or may not occur, with little to no research or knowledge. A speculator may do more homework and try to make an 'educated guess' on the outcome. A true investor, however, gathers pertinent data, analyzes the potential risks and rewards, and makes an informed decision based on the asset's past and likely future performance. An investor is less prone to be swayed by temporary market conditions and less inclined to make an emotional decision.

The Magic of Compound Interest and Leverage Combined

It's time to turn our attention back to compound interest. We've already seen the damage it can do if you're in debt, so now let's consider the flip side. Say you put the same
$5000 into a savings account, earning 5% per annum. At the end of the first year, you earn $250 in interest. If you take no further action and leave it to accumulate, earning interest on your interest as well as the principal, in the second year, you receive $262.50 interest on your
$5250. Afier five years, you have $6416 and afier 30 years, it's grown to $21,610.

The problem is, if inflation runs at an average of 3% over those 30 years, the spending power of your $21,610 in 30 years' time equates to just $8,957 in today's terms. That's before you take any taxes into consideration.

Now let's assume you want to increase your rate of return. You could invest your $5000 in stocks or bonds and if the market performs true to historical averages, achieve an average 8% return on investment. With most investments,
$5000 cash buys you $5000 worth of assets. That's where leverage comes in. Instead of using your $5000 to buy an equal amount worth of assets, you can use it as the down payment on a property worth
$100,000, with rental income of $12,000 per annum. Even with loan repayments of $450 per month at 4% and other operating costs around the same, you can still expect to clear $100 per month on the deal. That's a 24% annual rate of return on your original investment of $5000.

We discuss the different types of investment and their pros and cons in more detail later in the book. Suffice it to say for now, once you have savings in place to cover minor emergencies, and are ready to start investing, rental real estate is a smart first option to consider.

The Importance of Multiple Streams of Income vs. Diversification.

Before we move on to considering the principles of investing and what to look for in a good investment, let me clarify another aspect of investing that causes confusion for many new investors. This stems from two pieces of advice related to risk management, which at first glance may seem to be the same but have important differences.

The first is the need to establish multiple streams of income. If your only source of income is your salary and you lose your job, you take a financial hit from which you might not recover. Even with own-occupation disability insurance, your policy will likely only pay out a percentage of your salary, and that only after an initial deferred period. If you have $50,000 to invest and you sink it all into stocks in just one company and that company goes bust, you lose your entire investment. Or if you own one building and it's made somehow uninhabitable, you lose your rental income overnight.

On the other hand, investing $5000 in ten different companies or leveraging your $50,000 to mortgage multiple rental properties lessens this type of risk. If one asset fails to earn the expected income, the others are unaffected, and your overall portfolio remains viable.

This kind of risk management is often confused with diversification, another strategy many new investors are advised to adopt. The true meaning of diversification, however, is splitting your portfolio and investing in different types of investment or asset classes. A portfolio that consists entirely of stocks, for example, is vulnerable to market crashes. One consisting of real estate in a tight geographical area is vulnerable to localized economic downturn, flood, fire, and other natural or manmade disaster. A diverse portfolio attempts to balance this risk using asset allocation and investing a set percentage of the overall amount into different vehicles. A cautious investor may hold 40% in bonds, 30% in stocks, and another 30% in real estate.

The danger in diversification comes when an inexperienced investor attempts to mitigate risk by investing too-small amounts in too many investment vehicles. With this approach, associated fees eat into and even engulf profits, leading to lower rates of return than those achievable on a more concentrated portfolio. A little diversification protects you from the vagaries of the financial industry. As is so often the case, though, too much of a good thing can be your downfall. As Warren Buffett is quoted as saying, "Wide diversification is only required when investors do not understand what they are doing."

"Games are won by players who focus on the playing field — not by those whose eyes are glued to the scoreboard."

Warren Buffet

Principles of Investing

I'm ready to start looking at investments, but I'm still not clear on how to evaluate different options. Can you give me some ground rules to keep in mind when considering investment opportunities?

You've heard the saying, "If you want success, model success." If you're looking for some sound basic principles to apply when considering investments, you could do a lot worse than to take a page from Warren Buffet's book. He seems to know a thing or two about making money. Buffet himself learned his investing acumen from his mentor Benjamin Graham, whose book, *The Intelligent Investor*, teaches three basic principles:

Margin of Safety

The first principle of investing, according to Graham, is to purchase an undervalued asset. Graham focused with laser precision on companies whose stocks were trading well below the company's liquidation value, aiming to buy stock at 50 cents on the dollar. Since these businesses were undervalued, he reasoned, they were likely to rebound to a fair market value rather than continue to fall. They were unlikely to fail, as they were asset rich and unencumbered by debts.

Profit from Volatility

If the Margin of Safety principle equates to advice to 'buy low,' Graham's second principle, Profit from Volatility, is the corresponding advice to 'sell high.' Graham likened the stock market to an emotionally unstable business partner who offers to sell you his stake in the business or buy yours daily. Yet the bid and offer prices swing wildly from one day to the next. Every day you are free to buy, sell, or ignore the offer.

Having invested based on value, Graham's only concern for 'Mr. Market' was the sell price, and he advised only selling when the market prices become dangerously or unsustainably high.

Know Yourself

If you have the time to devote to learning and researching individual businesses, become an active investor. If you don't, become a passive investor and invest in an index or syndication. For Graham, these were the two best choices. By mirroring an index, he pointed out, you could match its performance. But trying to outperform the market by applying just a little knowledge, he warned, more ofien results in more failure than success. Even the most knowledgeable fund managers had about as much chance of beating the market as winning a coin toss.

Graham counseled against the dangers of overconfidence and impatience, emphasizing the need to base decisions on empirical evidence and confidence to walk away from an investment if it didn't meet strict criteria. He placed a great deal of emphasis on the difference between speculating, which he likened to gambling, and investing, which he considered "an… operation… which, upon thorough analysis, promises safety of principal and a satisfactory return." While Graham acknowledged there is an element of speculation in all investment since there is always the possibility of loss, he warned against "unintelligent speculation," including:

- Speculating when you think you are investing.
- Speculating when you lack proper knowledge and skill for it.
- Risking more money than you can afford to lose.

Warren Buffet said no one ever lost money following Graham's principles, but that didn't prevent him from adapting them to suit his own needs.

Avoid Over-Diversification

Where Buffet differs from Graham is in his attitude toward diversification, choosing to concentrate on fewer stocks based on the quality of the underlying business. Graham advised investors to hold 10 - 30 different stocks. Buffet suggests an uninformed investor, unwilling to put in the time to research each company he considers investing in, should invest in index funds. A "know-something" investor, able to understand business economics and find five to ten sensibly priced companies with important long-term competitive advantages, does better to limit his holdings to those five to ten companies he believes in and has time to follow.⁵

Invest Long-Term

Perhaps one reason for Buffet's departure from Graham's methodology is his belief in long-term investment. Where Graham sold stock at a predetermined price, Buffet urges investors to slow down, make as few investments as possible and ignore market fluctuations. Focus instead on the long-term productivity and prospects of the business. He even says his preferred holding period is "forever." As he points out, every trade has associated fees and multiple trades eat into your portfolios profits.

Nevertheless, both individuals and institutions will constantly be urged to be active by those who profit from giving advice or effecting transactions. The resulting frictional costs can be huge and, for investors in aggregate, devoid of benefit. So, ignore the chatter, keep your costs minimal, and invest in stocks as you

Warren Buffet, 2014Annual Letter to Investors⁶

Use Leverage to Buy the Farm

Buffet also applies these principles to real estate investing and buying entire businesses, not just solely to stocks. Several commentators, including Lee Adler of *The Wall Street Examiner*, point out much of Buffet's spectacular

---

⁵ Berkshirehathaway.com,. 2016. "Chairman's Letter - 1993". http://www.berkshirehathaway.com/letters/1993.html.

⁶ Buffett, Warren. 2014. "Buffett'S Annual Letter: What You Can Learn From My Real Estate Investments". *Fortune.* http://fortune.com/2014/02/24/buffetts-annual-letter-what-you-can-learn-from-my-real-estate-investments/.

success is due to his ownership of insurance companies, and his ability to leverage the premiums paid by policyholders to generate larger returns than the average investor on a similar trade.[7]

In his 2014 Letter to Investors, Buffet discussed two real estate investments, one of which he made in partnership with a fellow investor who has more knowledge of the property and its attendant business. If Warren Buffet can team up with others to buy assets, so can you.

Just as managed funds allow small investors to spread the risk of investing in multiple companies by pooling their resources, crowdfunding real estate options and real estate syndicates do the same for small investors and are growing in popularity exponentially. They are a means for you to take advantage of the power of leverage to own rental real estate, while still limiting your investment and attendant risk.

We talk more about the power of leverage and the pros and cons of different financial vehicles in later chapters. First, let's focus on the importance of discipline and adopting a long-term attitude to investing.

---

[7] Adler, Lee. 2015. "Warren Buffett's Dirty Little Secret - Leverage And Speculation - The Wall Street Examiner". *The Wall Street Examiner*. http:/ wallstreetexaminer.com/2015/05/warren-buffetts-dirty-little-secret-leverage-and-speculation/.

"The most important quality for an investor is temperament, not intellect. You need a temperament that neither derives great pleasure from being with the crowd or against the crowd."

Warren Buffett

Discipline

I have a couple of small investments that gave me good returns. Now I want to use the money to pay for a vacation. Does that hurt my long-term savings?

When did you know you wanted to go into medicine? How many other kids did you know who wanted to be doctors? Lawyers? Professional sports players? Did all of them make it?

Chances are, you know at least one person who dropped out of medical school or who finished college and instead went into an associated profession, rather than continuing their studies to qualify for what they originally set their sights on.

Every year, 82% of medical school students graduate in four years; about 95% graduate within eight years.[8] Medicine is a tough discipline and not everyone can make it. To get where you are today, you made a commitment, you put in a lot of hours, you were determined, and you stuck with it.

It's the same with money. If you want to be a successful investor, you make the commitment, work on it, and stay focused on your goal.

The difference a few percentage points can make, and the advantages of time and timing, are integral components to your success.

By way of example, look at the PGA Tour's 2015 top earners. Jordan Speith ranked first with earnings of $9,170,215 from 20 events. He has an average score of 68.8 strokes per round. Billy Horschel, who ranked 23rd, has earnings of $1,532,813 from 23 events. His average score is 70.3. The difference in their scores is just 1% – but the difference in their earnings is $7,637,402. A difference of one single percentage point in golf strokes generated 83%

---

[8]Caulfield, Marie, Geoffrey Redden, and Henry Sondheimer. 2014. *Graduation Rates And Attrition Factors For U.S. Medical School Students*. Ebook. 1st ed. Washington, D.C: AAMC. https:/ www.aamc.org/download/379220/data/may2014aib-graduationratesandattritionfactorsforusmedschools.pdf.

higher earnings for Speith. Such is the power of a "few" percentage points.

Speith and other professional golfers are constantly concerned about peaking too soon. They wonder how to get the timing right to sustain and improve their performance throughout the season, like Horschel did so spectacularly in 2014. Successive wins that year at the BMW Championship and Coca-Cola TOUR Championship that year catapulted him from 45th to 14th in world rankings, landing him one spot behind #13 at the time, Jordan Speith.

In the ensuing year, Speith climbed steadily to take the number one spot, while Horschel sadly sank to 23rd. Their respective differences in earnings followed suit. These statistics are a sobering reminder that in the end, time is more powerful than timing.

Patience, determination, and steady application outperform short streaks of brilliance repeatedly. Remember those medical school graduation figures we talked about? For those who took non-joint degree research or a leave of absence, the graduation figures drop significantly to 51.5% in five years and 69.8% in eight years. That means taking a year off from medical school increases the chances of not graduating six-fold, from just 5% to 31%.

So, what does all of that have to do with investing? Go back to our $5000 example in Investing 101. There we saw that if lefi untouched in a savings account earning 5% interest for 30 years, our investment would grow to $21,610. The interest over the years would look something like this:

Year	Balance	Deposit	Interest %	Interest $
1	$ -	$5,000	5%	$ 250
2	$ 5,250	0	5%	$ 263
3	$ 5,513	0	5%	$ 276
4	$ 5,788	0	5%	$ 289
5	$ 6,078	0	5%	$ 304
6	$ 6,381	0	5%	$ 319

7	$ 6,700	0	5%	$ 335
8	$ 7,036	0	5%	$ 352
9	$ 7,387	0	5%	$ 369
10	$ 7,757	0	5%	$ 388
11	$ 8,144	0	5%	$ 407
12	$ 8,552	0	5%	$ 428
13	$ 8,979	0	5%	$ 449
14	$ 9,428	0	5%	$ 471
15	$ 9,900	0	5%	$ 495
16	$ 10,395	0	5%	$ 520
17	$ 10,914	0	5%	$ 546
18	$ 11,460	0	5%	$ 573
19	$ 12,033	0	5%	$ 602
20	$ 12,635	0	5%	$ 632
21	$ 13,266	0	5%	$ 663
22	$ 13,930	0	5%	$ 696
23	$ 14,626	0	5%	$ 731
24	$ 15,358	0	5%	$ 768
25	$ 16,125	0	5%	$ 806
26	$ 16,932	0	5%	$ 847
27	$ 17,778	0	5%	$ 889
28	$ 18,667	0	5%	$ 933
29	$ 19,601	0	5%	$ 980
30	$ 20,581	0	5%	$ 1,029
31	$ 21,610			

Now assume afier five years you withdraw your $5000 principal. What effect does that have on your previous
$21,610 total at the end of 30 years? Would you expect to walk away with $16,000? $10,000? Here's what would happen:

Year	Balance	Deposit	Interest %	Interest $
1	$ -	5000	5%	$ 250
2	$ 5,250	0	5%	$ 263
3	$ 5,513	0	5%	$ 276
4	$ 5,788	0	5%	$ 289

5	$ 6,078	0	5%	$ 304
6	$ 6,381	-5000	5%	$ 69
7	$ 1,450	0	5%	$ 73
8	$ 1,523	0	5%	$ 76
9	$ 1,599	0	5%	$ 80
10	$ 1,679	0	5%	$ 84
11	$ 1,763	0	5%	$ 88
12	$ 1,851	0	5%	$ 93
13	$ 1,944	0	5%	$ 97
14	$ 2,041	0	5%	$ 102
15	$ 2,143	0	5%	$ 107
16	$ 2,250	0	5%	$ 113
17	$ 2,363	0	5%	$ 118
18	$ 2,481	0	5%	$ 124
19	$ 2,605	0	5%	$ 130
20	$ 2,735	0	5%	$ 137
21	$ 2,872	0	5%	$ 144
22	$ 3,015	0	5%	$ 151
23	$ 3,166	0	5%	$ 158
24	$ 3,325	0	5%	$ 166
25	$ 3,491	0	5%	$ 175
26	$ 3,665	0	5%	$ 183
27	$ 3,849	0	5%	$ 192
28	$ 4,041	0	5%	$ 202
29	$ 4,243	0	5%	$ 212
30	$ 4,455	0	5%	$ 223
31	$ 4,678			

Afier the remaining 25 years, you're lefi with just $4687!

You didn't just spend the $5000; you lost the interest it would have earned you over those ensuing 25 years. That
We call that the power of lost opportunity.

What if you instead withdrew your principal $5000 after 25 years?

Year	Balance	Deposit	Interest %	Interest $
1	$ -	5000	5%	$ 250
2	$ 5,250	0	5%	$ 263
3	$ 5,513	0	5%	$ 276
4	$ 5,788	0	5%	$ 289
5	$ 6,078	0	5%	$ 304
6	$ 6,381	0	5%	$ 319
7	$ 6,700	0	5%	$ 335
8	$ 7,036	0	5%	$ 352
9	$ 7,387	0	5%	$ 369
10	$ 7,757	0	5%	$ 388
11	$ 8,144	0	5%	$ 407
12	$ 8,552	0	5%	$ 428
13	$ 8,979	0	5%	$ 449
14	$ 9,428	0	5%	$ 471
15	$ 9,900	0	5%	$ 495
16	$ 10,395	0	5%	$ 520
17	$ 10,914	0	5%	$ 546
18	$ 11,460	0	5%	$ 573
19	$ 12,033	0	5%	$ 602
20	$ 12,635	0	5%	$ 632
21	$ 13,266	0	5%	$ 663
22	$ 13,930	0	5%	$ 696
23	$ 14,626	0	5%	$ 731
24	$ 15,358	0	5%	$ 768
25	$ 16,125	-5000	5%	$ 556
26	$ 11,682	0	5%	$ 584
27	$ 12,266	0	5%	$ 613
28	$ 12,879	0	5%	$ 644
29	$ 13,523	0	5%	$ 676
30	$ 14,199	0	5%	$ 710
31	$ 14,909			

Yoe54ru still have almost $15,000 earned in interest!

That is the power of time and the importance of timing working in your favor. It's why you need to choose investments with the long term in mind and stick to your plan.

I'm not saying put all your money into a savings account. As we've already seen, there are much more effective ways to put your money to work. In coming chapters, we'll look at some of the different financial vehicles and their pros and cons. First, though, learn a quick trick to calculate returns on investment as we investigate the power of percentages a little closer.

"Successful investing takes time, discipline, and patience. No matter how great the talent or effort, some things just take time: You can't produce a baby in one month by getting nine women pregnant"

Warren Buffett

Understanding Rates of Return

"I've heard that stocks historically outperform other investments over the long term, but I've made some bad investments in the past and lost large chunks of my portfolio in market crashes. I read somewhere that pundits expect the market to produce returns between 10 - 20% per year and I could double my money every five years. Is that true?"

There are three factors at work here. An additional consideration – the all-too human tendency to overestimate future returns – comes up later in a separate section. Here, I want to focus solely on the effects of percentages on growth rates and the inherent danger in using historical averages to predict future performance.

Rule of 72

There's a neat trick that investors use to calculate how long it takes to double an investment at a given rate of return. It's called the Rule of 72. It's calculated based on the length of time it would take a dollar (or any other amount) to double by increasing at 1% per period. In most cases this would be years, but in short-term deals the period may be months, or even days.

The actual number is 69.3, but it's rounded to 72 as the nearest number that has the most divisible factors[9]. The Rule of 72 works because the length of time it takes to double your money alters in inverse proportion to how much the interest rate fluctuates from the base by 1%. If the rate is 2%, your dollar doubles in half the time, or 36 periods. Increase it to 3%, and the time to double falls to 24 periods, and so on.

You can also use the Rule of 72 in reverse to calculate the interest rate you must secure to double your money in a certain length of time. Similarly, you can determine how long it takes to triple or quadruple your money. In fact, you can use it to calculate how long it takes to increase your money by any factor. Keep in mind, however, that the higher percentage rate of return, the less accurate these mental divisions will be.

The simplest way to demonstrate how the Rule of 72 works is to give you a chart showing the time required to increase your money by certain factors at specific interest rates. I included on the chart heading the "rough and ready" numbers to use in each case. You can see a more complete table with a wider range of interest rates and multiplication factors at FinancialWellnessMD.com.

---

[9] Betterexplained.com,. 2016. "The Rule Of 72 | Betterexplained". http:/ betterexplained.com/articles/the-rule-of-72/.

Factor	x2	x3	x4	x5	x6	x8	x10
Annualized Interest rate	#Periods to increase investment by factor						
.5%	140	220	278	322	360	416	462
1%	70	110	139	161	180	208	231
2%	35	55	69.5	80.5	90	104	115.5
3%	23.3	36.7	46.3	53.7	60	69.3	77
4%	17.5	27.5	34.8	40.3	45	52	57.8
5%	14	22	27.8	32.2	36	41.6	46.2
6%	11.7	18.3	23.2	26.8	30	34.7	38.5
7%	10	15.7	19.9	23	25.7	29.7	33
8%	8.8	13.8	17.4	20.1	22.5	26	28.9
9%	7.8	12.2	15.4	17.9	20	23.1	25.7
10%	7	11	13.9	16.1	18	20.8	23.1
12%	5.8	9.2	11.6	13.4	15	17.3	19.3
14%	5	7.9	9.9	11.5	12.9	14.9	16.5
16%	4.4	6.9	8.7	10.1	11.3	13	14.4
18%	3.9	6.1	7.7	8.9	10	11.6	12.8
20%	3.5	5.5	7	8.1	9	10.4	11.6

The Rule of 72 reveals how much more money you make (or how much less time it takes to double) by securing even 1% more (or less). Using the same $5000 from previous examples, compare the 5% savings account with an investment account returning a single percentage point more:

At 5%, it takes 14 years to double your money and at the end of the 30-year experiment, you are still more than two years away from achieving $25,000. As we've already seen, you still have $21,610.

At 6%, you double your money in 11.7 years. At the end of the 30 years you haven't simply multiplied your money by five, you approach a six-fold increase.

The moral of this story is to maximize the rate of return. This comes with a caveat, though: Don't be seduced by historical averages.

The Danger of Historical Averages

I don't want to condemn stocks as a viable part of a balanced portfolio. That's not what this chapter is about. Understand that the principles discussed here in relation to stocks also apply to other types of investment. I'm using stocks as an example because they are publicly traded and that makes historical data relatively easy to acquire.

These figures from the NYU Stern website show the actual performance of the Standard & Poor's 500 over the past 30 years[10]. In 1985, it wasn't hard to find pundits predicting future percentage rates of return in the high teens. As a conservative illustration, say you invested that exemplary $5000 in an index fund matching the S&P 500 back then. You might forecast, given an average 15% rate of return, you'd have returns in the region of $330,000. Go ahead and take a moment to soak that in.

$ 5,000	Predicted 15%	Actual Rates	Actual Return	Average Return
1985	$5,750.00	31.24%	$6,562.00	$5,635.00
1986	$6,612.50	18.49%	$7,775.31	$6,350.65
1987	$7,604.38	5.81%	$8,227.06	$7,157.18
1988	$8,745.03	16.54%	$9,587.82	$8,066.14
1989	$10,056.79	31.48%	$12,606.06	$9,090.54
1990	$11,565.30	-3.06%	$12,220.31	$10,245.04

[10] Pages.stern.nyu.edu,. 2016. http:/ pages.stern.nyu.edu/~adamodar/New_Home_Page/datafile/histretSP.html.

1991	$13,300.10	30.23%	$15,914.51	$11,546.16
1992	$15,295.11	7.49%	$17,106.51	$13,012.52
1993	$17,589.38	9.97%	$18,812.03	$14,665.11
1994	$20,227.79	1.33%	$19,062.23	$16,527.58
1995	$23,261.96	37.20%	$26,153.38	$18,626.58
1996	$26,751.25	22.68%	$32,084.97	$20,992.15
1997	$30,763.94	33.10%	$42,705.09	$23,658.16
1998	$35,378.53	28.34%	$54,807.72	$26,662.74
1999	$40,685.31	20.89%	$66,257.05	$30,048.91
2000	$46,788.10	-9.03%	$60,274.04	$33,865.12
2001	$53,806.32	-11.85%	$53,131.56	$38,165.99
2002	$61,877.27	-21.97%	$41,458.56	$43,013.08
2003	$71,158.86	28.36%	$53,216.21	$48,475.74
2004	$81,832.69	10.74%	$58,931.63	$54,632.15
2005	$94,107.59	4.83%	$61,778.02	$61,570.44
2006	$108,223.73	15.61%	$71,421.57	$69,389.88
2007	$124,457.29	5.48%	$75,335.48	$78,202.40
2008	$143,125.88	-36.55%	$47,800.36	$88,134.10
2009	$164,594.76	25.94%	$60,199.77	$99,327.13
2010	$189,283.98	14.82%	$69,121.38	$111,941.68
2011	$217,676.57	2.10%	$70,572.93	$126,158.27
2012	$250,328.06	15.89%	$81,786.97	$142,180.37
2013	$287,877.27	32.15%	$108,081.48	$160,237.28
2014	$331,058.86	13.48%	$122,650.86	$180,587.42
		381.73%	122.650.86-$5,000	

S&P 500 Historical Performance 1985 - 2014

The actual annualized average Rate of Return (RoR) over those 30 years was closer to 12.7%. You might think 2.3% underperformance isn't so bad and expect losing around
$7600 on the deal. Afier all, that's around 2.3% of $330,000, right?

Look closer. The chart shows how a 2.3% underperformance over 30 years results in a portfolio value of around $180,000, a staggering drop in excess of 45%.

If you understand the principle of compound interest, that doesn't come as too much of a shock. Instead of doubling your money in 1989 as predicted, you would pass the magic $10,000 a year later in 1990. Instead of passing the factor X10 in 2006, you must wait until 2010.

Notice, though, how the actual performance figures based on the annual performance rates are even worse. Despite having doubled your money earlier than predicted, you must wait for a painstaking seventeen more years to pass the $100,000 mark. Instead of your expected $330,000 – or even the disappointing $180,000 – you have only
$122,650 in your portfolio afier 30 years. And that's before the effects of inflation and taxes are taken into consideration.

It's vital to understand the difference between performance forecasts based on historical averages and figures based on the compound effect of those same results.

We call this the net Compound Annual Growth Rate (CAGR.) Here's how it's calculated:

- Divide the value of an investment at the end of the period by its value at the beginning of that period.
- Multiply the result by a power of one divided by the period length.
- Subtract one from the result.

In this example using the $5000, it looks like this:

($122,650.86/$5000)$^{(1/30)}$ - 1 which equates to a CGR of 11.26%.

Note: You don't need to learn the formula, it's included here for educational purposes. Just visit FinancialWellnessMD.com and use our investment calculators.

If anyone shows you a prediction based on the average RoR of an investment, ask what the CAGR is. While that can't guarantee your investment is safe from loss, it at least gives you a more realistic expectation of future results.

"It is important for investors to understand what they do and don't know. Learn to recognize that you cannot possibly know what is going to happen in the future, and any investment plan that is dependent on accurately forecasting where markets will be next year is doomed to failure."

Barry Ritholtz

What You Know

I've dabbled with investing in stocks and shares in the past, with mixed success. It seems someone always has a hot tip that's too good to pass up. Sometimes they pan out. Others, I've got the timing wrong and ended up wiping out my gains and even losing money. How can I avoid hopping from one 'surefire' investment to another? I've heard I should invest in what I know, but I don't know anything about the financial market. Does that mean I should only invest in pharmaceuticals?

The advice to invest in what you know is designed to prevent inexperienced investors from plunging their money into high-risk start-ups or fast-growth companies whose business models they don't understand. The theory goes that if you know enough about a company to at least explain how it makes money, you should also be able to read the warning signs and steer clear of an enterprise that's destined to fail and take your money with it.

The problem is that what most people know about are the big, safe companies. Corporations like Wells Fargo, Coca-Cola, IBM, American Express, and Wal-Mart sit at the top of Warren Buffett's Berkshire Hathaway fund because they are established businesses unlikely to generate huge losses. And residential rental property is the investment of choice for many new real estate investors because it's also familiar, closest to mortgaging or renting your own home. It feels like a safe option.

Two challenges arise with these types of investments.

First, because they are popular and considered safe bets, everyone wants them. The barriers to entry can be high. At the time of writing, those five stocks are trading between $42.68 and $140.30 per share. And if you want to buy residential real estate rental property, you need a down payment, plus enough to cover legal fees, landlord insurance, and other associated costs.

Second, even large, safe companies are subject to the vagaries of the market. Over the course of the past year, IBM, American Express, and Wal-Mart shares have all dropped significantly in value, with Wells Fargo and Coca-Cola holding steady. Does this make them bad investments? No. Chances are they will rebound, and the long-term investor is more concerned with dividends than with fluctuations in market price. But the inexperienced investor may panic and jump ship when the investments fall a few points, creating unnecessary losses and the conviction that even solid investments are too risky.

A new landlord, when tallying end-of-year accounts that show a loss, might panic and sell up (incurring further costs), rather than understanding legal fees can eat into early profits and prepare for it for it. This investor might conclude that real estate is not for him. Chances are, he didn't make a bad investment, he just gave up too soon.

An even bigger problem with this invest-in-what-you-know attitude is that by limiting your chance to invest in higher-earning opportunities, it inhibits your power to create a balanced portfolio.

Without investment dollars fueling new ideas, architects might not have CAD sofiware for their designs; airline pilots might not have pinpoint, fly-by-wire navigation systems; attorneys might not have efficient sofiware for their legal work; and the medical field might not have advances in fighting illness and disease that improve quality of life across the board.

In the same way, without real estate development, communities become static and fall into decline. The Wal-Mart formula demonstrates this in commercial real estate. Where Wal-Mart goes, so goes Home Depot, Staples, Michael's Crafis, CVS, and a long line of other merchant retailers. Soon come the land developers to build communities, parks, schools, churches, medical buildings, hospitals, and the like. Then comes the supporting labor force – who may not be able to afford the homes being built but needs apartments – so then come the contractors to build these dwellings and more affordable businesses to support this large consumer sector.

Everywhere we look, including the mobile miracle in our hands that can call people around the world from almost any location — investment dollars advance society. From an investment point of view, it's those potentially risky startups that have the greatest growth outlook. The trick is understanding what you're getting into and having realistic expectations.

While invest-in-what-you-know is not bad advice, I prefer to turn that sentence on its head and say, *"Know what you're investing in."* Instead of imitating others and trying to spot trends, develop long-term strategies of your own.

You don't prescribe a new drug or perform a new procedure without first reading the literature and doing your research. You don't prescribe every patient the same drug or treat them only according to your expertise while ignoring their condition. You must bring to investing that same intelligence, level of discernment, and willingness to do your homework.

When you look at any investment opportunity, look beyond the headline figures. Ask questions about what those figures are based on. Consider the underlying business and assets. Understand the current cost-to-value proposition.

Don't follow the crowd or be swayed by a slick sales pitch. If you're investing in a business, look at the people running the company. What is their track record? The same applies to builders and new builds.

If you look at existing real estate, consider property and rental values in the area, the reputation of the management company. If you invest through a broker-dealer or advisor of any kind, understand the fees and commissions involved, and how they affect your returns.

Do your research. Take it all into account so you can measure potential return, your own risk tolerance, and how much you're willing to invest in that opportunity. If your instinct is to walk away, do. There is never a shortage of opportunities.

"Economics is all about consumption. People either spend money now or they use financial instruments - like bonds, stocks, and savings accounts - so they can spend more later."

Adam Davidson

Financial Vehicles

Jocelyn Ibanez-Pantaleon, MD

Medical Writer and Fitness Blogger
Owner/Resident Physician, Pantaleon Polyclinic

http://globalmedicalwriting.com

"I've got a healthy buffer built up in my savings account for contingencies. Now I'm ready to start investing with an eye to building up my nest egg for the future and creating a residual income. Should I put everything into stocks and bonds, and if not, what are my other options?"

When thinking about investing, most people think first of the stock market, as that gets the most media coverage. It pays to remember, though, that it gets so much coverage because of its volatility and because with it comes the risk of enormous losses as well as significant gains.

What appears below goes from the basics of banking instruments to more sophisticated things to consider, as financial planners ofien present financial instruments in this order of increasing risk and potential return.

Savings Account

A savings account is a bank account that provides principal security and modest interest earnings. It used to be a lousy way of earning some cash for your money stash and may remind you about your grandma always carrying her passbook with her for her financial convenience. With the modern introduction of online bank accounts that offer bonuses and high interest rates, saving through these accounts became popular once again. Although there are other higher-yielding ways to make your money work for you, a savings account is a safe option for keeping some cash as your emergency fund.

Certificate of Deposit

If you are looking for other ways to earn more money than a regular savings account, placing funds into a certificate of deposit is something to consider. Remember – inflation tends to run higher than interest paid on most CDs — so let's call it another savings instrument NOT an investment. Several banks offer a higher yield for your investment than a savings account, but there is a caveat: The bank keeps your money for a certain period. Withdrawing your money before the agreed date means paying a penalty in lost interest.

Annuities

An annuity is another financial savings vehicle. When you buy an annuity, you agree to pay a fixed amount to the financial institution at regular time intervals, usually monthly or annually. The institution invests on your behalf, with the promise of a regular income at the end of the fixed term. Annuities secured in the form of pensions can ensure a reliable cash flow in later, i.e., retirement years. This goes a long way to alleviate fears of outliving your assets or increased longevity risks. Although an annuity is a great way to save money for future use, one of its disadvantages is its lack of liquidity. Just like the certificate of deposit, annuities are locked in for a certain period and touching your money before the expiration of the agreed time means you pay a penalty. The penalties for early withdrawal or cash-in on annuities are ofien much higher than CDs and can completely wipe out any financial gain.

Mutual Funds

A mutual fund is a managed investment program that aims to trade diversified holdings such as bonds, stocks, money market instruments, and other similar assets. One of the greatest advantages of securing a mutual fund is the opportunity to access a professionally managed form of financial security. Just like other financial vehicles, though, securing a mutual fund also carries some risks. Each shareholder participates proportionally in the gains of the mutual fund, but he or she also participates proportionally in any loss of such a fund.

Stocks

A stock is a type of financial security that represents a claim on a part of a corporation's earnings and assets. Your corporate ownership percentage is determined by the number of shares you have in relation to the number of outstanding shares the entire corporation has. As with mutual funds, owning a stock or share in a corporation means participating proportionally in the gains or loss of the corporation.

Life Insurance

Life insurance is a contract between the insured person – who pays a premium – and an insurance provider – which receives the premium. It aims to pay the designated beneficiary a sum of money upon the death of the insured. Depending on the contract, other events such as critical illness or terminal disease can also trigger the release of payment from the insurance company.

Disability Insurance

Disability insurance is another form of financial security intended to protect the beneficiary's earned income against possible disability that creates a barrier to executing the core functions of his or her work. Disability insurance is a great way to secure your earnings in case of long-term health problems. Nevertheless, it is not a 100% perfect plan. High-limit disability plans can only pay up to 65% of the beneficiary's income, regardless of income level.

Long-Term Care Insurance

Long-term care insurance is yet another form of insurance that helps provide for the expenses of long-term care beyond a predetermined period that are not covered by health insurance, Medicaid, or Medicare. Long-term care insurances are designed to regularly reimburse a set amount to assist their policyholders in availing themselves of services to support their daily living activities such as eating, bathing, and dressing.

Real Estate Investment

Investing in real estate is an increasingly popular investment and during the last fifiy years it can offer bigger and brighter opportunity of greater gains compared to other forms of investments. Choosing and buying the right real estate is a lot more complicated than simply opening a savings account or buying a certificate of deposit from your local bank.

Real estate is a very profitable business. You ofien need to make certain tweaks to turn your real estate into an income-generating investment. These tweaks can include:

- Converting your real estate to a basic rental property.
- Joining a real estate investment group and letting the company manage your property and create profits for you.
- Trading in real estate by selling it for a profit when it increases in value.

Alternative Assets

You can also invest in alternative asset classes, such as precious metals, promissory notes, tax liens, hedge funds, private equity, or direct ownership of businesses. These are typically considered high-risk and high-reward. You might add these to your portfolio once you are comfortable with investing in general, but they rarely make a good choice for inexperienced investors.

Amir Says

Thank you, Jocelyn, for giving us a quick rundown on the basic types of investments available, and for highlighting the difference between saving and investing. Savings accounts in general are not designed to increase your net worth in relative terms over time; their aim is simply to negate the effects of inflation so that your money has the same spending power when you withdraw it as when you deposit. With online high-yield savings accounts currently offering competitive interest rates, it's probably better to just have the cash on hand than tie up your money for as much as four years in a comparable-earning CD. High-yield savings accounts generally allow up to six withdrawals per month without incurring any penalties in lost interest.

When looking into stocks, it's worth bearing in mind the concept of control. If you buy a small number of shares in a large company, you have no control over how the board members manage the company. You may gain voting rights at the annual general meeting, but your voice is just one of many. If you disagree with the business's decisions, your only option is to sell your stock. If the business tanks, you have no collateral. Shareholders, as equity holders, rank last in the order of creditors paid in case of liquidation.

If you're considering investing in stocks and don't have the time or capital to invest enough in a single company to gain at least some control over the business, it's probably better to invest in an index fund. Index funds are designed to follow the broader market, with little if any human intervention. This eliminates the fund manager's cost. As we discover in the chapter ahead on risk assessment, fund managers in general have a poor track record of outperforming the market, thereby ofien detracting from the fund's value twice over.

We also delve into insurance and the vital importance of own-occupation disability insurance in more detail in a later chapter. For now, it's time to take a closer look at real estate as an investment option.

"We are in the real estate business, not the hamburger business."

Ray Kroc

Real Estate

"I've had mixed results from my stock portfolio and heard real estate outperforms other investments over the long term. How can I get into it? What do I need to think about when evaluating a real estate deal?"

> According to The Land Report editor Eric O'Keefe,
> today about 80% of U.S. citizens live on just 3% of the land,
> with the greatest concentration in larger cities and urban areas.
> The top 100 private landowners between them own 33 million-plus
> of America's 2.3 billion acres.
> Even accounting for the 640 million or so acres
> owned and managed federally, these figures show
> there's a whole lot of land still available
> for acquisition, development, and profit.

Throughout history, land ownership has been a source of political power and one of the surest ways to wealth. America was founded on the principles of private property under a free market.[11] No fewer than <u>six</u> of the founding state's Declaration of Rights include either as the first article or in the preamble, the inherent right of all men to acquire, possess, and protect property.[12]

Of course, while all men and women may be created equal, all land is not. Real estate investment requires a dedicated and knowledgeable approach. Contrary to popular belief, simply investing in land or property with no clear objective or purpose does not automatically bring you profits.

---

[11] The Heritage Foundation,. 2010. "The Economic Principles Of America'S Founders: Property Rights, Free Markets, And Sound Money".
http:/ www.heritage.org/research/reports/2010/08/the-economic-principles-of-america-s-founders-property-rights-free-markets-and-sound-money.

[12] Declarations of Rights of Virginia, 1776, Art. 1, Pennsylvania, 1776, Art. 1; Vermont, 1777, Art. 1; Massachusetts, 1780, Art. 1; New Hampshire, 1784, Art. 2. Delaware, 1792, Preamble, has "acquiring and protecting reputation and property."

Investing in real estate directly or through funds or real estate investment trusts can add much-needed diversification to your investment portfolio. You can't ensure against stocks losing value without getting into complicated hedge funds and futures options. Real estate is underpinned by the intrinsic value of the land, though, and with the right insurance you can recoup your losses and redevelop should disaster strike.

There are always certain financial elements at play during an income-producing real estate investment. At all stages of the process understanding these essential metrics makes a huge difference in your returns. Be aware that real estate is a unique investment, so you cannot apply the same rules here as you do to investing in stocks or bonds.

These are seven rules of thumb that can help every investor:

Vacancy Rates

If you're looking at rental real estate, whether residential or commercial, you need to consider the vacancy rate of both the property in question and the surrounding area. Vacant units represent potential for increased income but also higher costs. While some vacancy may be desirable if you're confident you can rent out the space, higher vacancy suggests the rent amounts are too high for the location. High vacancy rates in the entire area may point to a community in decline – or one ripe for redevelopment.

New Construction vs. Existing Establishment Investment

Investing in new construction can be lucrative, with the potential to buy into new development at low rates and resell closer to market value, even during the construction phase. With a new build, you can also tailor the property to meet your needs, rather than retrofitting an existing building. You can also determine which amenities are installed, and deal with only the construction company in terms of land title and legalities.

On the downside, delays in construction and unexpected costs can and do occur, so check past projects and the reputation of the construction company before signing anything or handing over the first installment.

Whether investing in new or existing construction, carry out several checks to ensure there are no restrictions that would prevent your intended land use. These include but are not restricted to:

- Encumbrances such as liens (debts held against the land or property which may transfer to you as the new owner, including outstanding taxes and dues),
- Easements (rights of access by third parties),
- Profits-à-Prendre (rights to take something from the land such as mining or mineral rights)
- Encroachments, (extensions of physical structures such as buildings, fences, or trees from adjoining properties over the property lines)

Existing properties come with an additional set of considerations. Always check legal documents for clear title and consider recent survey and appraisal reports to avoid unexpected maintenance and repair costs. Consider the rental conditions of existing tenants: Is it rent-controlled, rent-stabilized or free market? Is the lease about to expire? Does it have renewal options in favor of the tenant? Are interior items owned by the tenant or the property owner? Quality-check items (furniture, fixtures, and equipment) if they are included in the sale.

Loan-To-Value Ratio (LTV)

When you buy a property for an income-based real estate investment, it's unlikely you pay cash or use all your own income. Most of the time, you apply for a mortgage on the property to take advantage of the power of leverage as we discussed earlier. This brings another metric into play – the Loan-To-Value Ratio (LTV).

Think of the LTV of a property as the flip side of your down payment. If you make an initial down payment on the investment, money from your own pocket of say 30%, then you will have an LTV of 70%.

Generally, lenders are only willing to finance between 60% and 80% of the appraised value of the property, so you must make a substantial down payment.

The lesson to learn here is that a higher LTV is less favorable than a lower one. A higher LTV means a higher risk, and incurs less advantageous terms on the mortgage, in the form of higher interest rates and fees. This all cuts directly into your returns. On the other hand, a higher LTV allows for higher leveraging, which can mean higher cash-on-cash returns on your money.

If you can put down a larger down payment, then do. This gives you a lower LTV, and the chance to secure the best rates on your mortgage, and therefore the best returns on your real estate.

Debt Coverage Ratio (DCR)

The debt coverage ratio (DCR) expresses the relationship between your Net Operating Income (NOI) and your Annual Debt Service (ADS). Your NOI is the amount of potential income a property can make, minus vacancy, credit loss (both covered above), and operating expenses. Your Annual Debt Service refers to the amount you pay on your mortgage.

If your NOI only just covers your mortgage, then your DCR is one, and you make no profit on the investment unless something changes. Lenders also use the DCR to weigh the risk of your investment. Generally, a DCR of at least 1.2 is required for lenders to consider putting up the money.

When looking for a mortgage there are a few things to consider:

- What type of mortgage best suits your plans? Fixed or variable rate? Interest-only or repayment mortgage? Fixed rates and repayment mortgages offer some security because you know in advance what your outgoings are, and you slowly bring down the outstanding balance. If you intend to retain the property indefinitely, consider paying it off over time. If, instead, you plan to sell in more favorable market conditions, you may prefer an interest-only loan.

- When financing or refinancing, pay close attention to the fees, terms and conditions, and possible charges associated with the loan. Know how much commission your broker receives and factor all costs into loan comparisons.

- Always hunt for the best deal. In addition to seeking lower interest rates, look for lower insurance premiums or processing charges waivers wherever possible.

Capitalization Rate

The Capitalization Rate (cap rate) of a property is the relationship between its NOI and its actual value. The cap rate is the ratio of a property's market value achieved in net income annually. For example, if a property has a value of
$100,000 and you make $10,000 from it afier costs, then the cap rate is 10%. You make a 10% return on your investment every year.

Cap rates are used by property appraisers to estimate the true value of a property. Before investing in any property, calculate the current cap rate of the property and talk to commercial real estate brokers in the area to work out the typical cap rate of other nearby commercial properties.

This gives you an idea whether the investment is underperforming, and thus has potential for improvement, or is at peak performance with less chance of increasing the NOI in the short term.

It is also useful to predict the future cap rate to see what to expect from the resale of the property. Bear in mind that cap rates fluctuate along with market conditions.

Internal Rate of Return (IRR)

Every investor wants to measure what he or she can expect from any given opportunity. You were already introduced to the NOI, which gives you a measure of the amount of income you can expect from your real estate afier expenses. The Internal Rate of Return (IRR) is an even more powerful metric you can use to gauge whether an investment is worth your while.

IRR is an estimate of the potential returns on an investment over time. It works on the premise that a dollar today is worth more than a dollar tomorrow due to effects of inflation, lost opportunity to gain interest on money not yet received, and the risk that expected income may not materialize. To achieve this, IRR uses a reverse calculation of compound interest, called "discounting," to arrive at a zero rate of present net value. There is no simple formula to calculate IRR. It's based on reversionary calculations, but modern spreadsheet sofiware (like Excel) has these built in, making finding IRR a simple matter once income and costs are established.

To be effective, estimate your future income and costs with reasonable accuracy. The result is the real return you achieve on a given property if all your assumptions are correct. Of course, no one has a crystal ball and unexpected costs, or loss of income naturally affect the actual returns, but this is true of any investment, regardless of the asset class.

Another drawback of IRR is that there is no ideal value. In simple terms, a higher risk should be rewarded with a higher IRR, but a high IRR estimate is also a sign that you have underestimated costs and overestimated income and capital gains on the property. While IRR is a valuable consideration to include in property evaluations, as always, question the source of the figures used to calculate it and revise it based on your own estimation before relying on it for decision making.

Cash flow

The final key rule for real estate investors takes us back to basics: cash flow. Cash is of utmost importance when seeking to invest. It's one thing to demonstrate that your property can show a positive NOI, quite another to ensure you have the necessary funds on hand at the right time. If you must undertake renovation before rental income can be obtained, you need more cash on hand earlier in the investment in addition to the down payment. If you have partially vacant property and you rely on current income to fund improvements and generate higher rents later, how do you cope if the vacancy rate increases and income decreases?

A negative cash flow can have you raiding your savings whenever anything unexpected happens and it leaves you in a poor position to make wise investment decisions. With a projection of positive cash flow, you can begin to measure the long-term potential of your investment. If the property rises in value, you may sell it for a handsome return, but if the bulk of your projected portfolio growth rests on increasing property prices and the market sinks, you need a healthy rental income to ride out the storm.

If all the talk of NOI, cap rates, and IRR leaves your eyes glazed over, consider partnering with someone who has residential or commercial real estate investing experience. In much the same way you might invest in an index fund rather than pick your own stocks, you are assured of due diligence and can mitigate the risk associated with potentially lucrative developments.

You can also take advantage of syndication real estate investment sites, such as FinancialwellnessMD.com. These allow smaller investors to gain access to more profitable deals traditionally reserved for large trusts and corporations, while simultaneously lowering the cost of entry and helping investors spread the risk across multiple projects.

Alpha Risk

"I've been building my portfolio for a while now and I have a few safe investments, but they are slow-growing. I know I need to balance my assets for growth, and I'm considering investing in real estate, but I'm worried about the high risk that comes with the potential for higher rewards. I heard about alpha and beta scores used to measure risk, but I don't know what they mean. Can you explain them?"

Thinking about risk as the potential for deviation from expectations, and rewards as potential return is a useful place to start.

If you remember the chapter "Understanding Rates of Return," where we discussed the compound annual growth rate (CAGR), think of that as the potential reward. In our example, the CAGR was 11.2%. With a high of 37.2% and a low of 36.55%, though, there is a lot of deviation from the mean. That represents the risk. Like the girl with a curl in the middle of her forehead, the good years can be very good, but the bad years can be horrid.

The holy grail of investing is finding an investment that consistently offers a high CAGR with minimal deviation from the norm, so that even years of poor performance have limited negative impact on the overall performance of the asset over time.

The stock market attempts to quantify these two aspects of risk and reward in terms of Alpha and Beta. Sort of.

The Alpha risk assessment is an evaluation of a fund manager's performance against the benchmark of the wider market. If his portfolio has outperformed the benchmark by 2%, he will have an alpha score of 2.0. If his returns trail the market by 1%, his fund's alpha score will be 1.5. So, a positive alpha score denotes a competent manager, and the higher the alpha score the better.

The Beta coefficient compares an asset's volatility over a given time to the same benchmark of the wider market. It works a little differently than the alpha score, in that the baseline score is one rather than zero. A score of less than one suggests the asset experiences less volatility than the benchmark average. Thus, the ideal is to find a fund with an alpha score as high as possible, and with a beta score as low as possible or at least below one.

A problem arises when attempting to use these stock market risk measurement tools with other asset classes, such as real estate or venture capitalism. This is partly to do with the problem of benchmarking and partly due to a necessary factor missing from stock market investments.

If you consider the benchmark issue first, a simple flaw is plain. Michael Jensen devised the alpha score in 1968 to determine fund managers' performance. Since the benchmark in question is the amalgamation of all fund managers' performances, it's a zero-sum game. Where losses offset gains, and they cancel each other out, it's not surprising to find that few fund managers achieve consistent, positive, let alone high alpha scores.

This norm of low and even negative alpha scores on the stock market leads to suspicion and skepticism when claims of consistently high alpha scores of multiple funds appear in other asset classes like real estate. But the benchmarks used in these classes are not merely the sum of all fund managers' results; they include results from assets beyond the scope of fund managers, including single properties in the same asset class not managed by a fund. Fund managers are being measured against not only other fund managers but all property owners in that asset class, the results of all included properties may cancel each other out, but the results of managed fund properties do not, making consistently higher alpha scores not only possible, but common.

The difference in alpha scores across markets is partially explained by the choice of benchmark and quality of data available upon which to base calculations.

Ronald W. Kaiser of Bailard, Inc., postulates an interesting theory of a third factor at play previously unaccounted for [13]. That factor, which Kaiser terms Gamma, is the ability to take control of the asset, and thus to generate value. While this gamma concept is in its infancy, Kaiser suggests revising the traditional equations of calculating portfolio performance from this:

Portfolio return = beta (market return) + alpha (manager selection and timing contribution)

to this:

Portfolio return = beta (market return) + alpha (selection, timing) + gamma (value-added)

He breaks down Beta, Alpha, and Gamma acts at portfolio and property level as described in the table following.

---

[13] Kaiser, Ronald W. 2005. *Analyzing Real Estate Portfolio Returns: More Than Alpha And Beta...There'S Gamma* . Ebook. 1st ed. Foster City, CA: Bailard, Inc. http:/ www.bailard.com/pdf/BeyondAlphaThere'sGamma.pdf.

These Gamma acts, he says, can also be classified as physical, financial, and operational activities that bring added value to the portfolio.

This explains why you shouldn't compare alpha scores, and to a lesser extent beta scores of stock market funds to those of property managers or venture capital funds. Until reliable benchmarks are established that account for varying levels of asset control, and gamma scores are widely accepted and factored into the equation, property funds continue to post higher scores. *Remember always: Compare like with like.*

	Beta	Alpha	Gamma
Portfolio Level	Implement client Benchmark Focus on adequate diversification. Add leverage to the portfolio.	Deviations from benchmark. Targeted over/under weights. Vary targets over the cycle. Vary leverage over the cycle. Timing of cash vs property.	Creative application of leverage strategies
Property Level	Buy core at market. Long term hold strategy.	Seek information advantage. Seek mispricing opportunities. Local cycle-timing strategies. Active high-bidder sales strategy.	Develop relationships to encourage owners to sell/joint venture "off market." Acquire properties with high vacancy risk. Property Control Activities: Control management/leasing team. Add developer partners to the team. Re-tenanting strategies. Refurbishment Redevelopment or new strategies development strategies.

"Investing should be more like watching paint dry or watching grass grow. If you want excitement, take $800 and go to Las Vegas."

Paul Samuelson

Long-Term Investment Guide

"Okay. I understand the need to focus on long-term investment and build a balanced portfolio for both consolidation and growth, but what does that look like? Can you tell me how much to invest and where?"

The short answer is, without in-depth analysis of your personal circumstances, goals and risk tolerance, no one can give you a simple formula to create a balanced portfolio that meets your specific needs. A good rule of thumb is to build a savings buffer in a high-yield savings account, get insurance in place to protect your current income, then spread your investments between large-cap stocks that pay reliable dividends and other asset classes with potential for greater growth. Only you can decide how big a buffer you need, the amount and type of insurance you can afford, and the proportion of safe but low-return investments vs. more volatile markets that represent a good fit for you.

We already talked about the need for discipline and for focusing on the long term rather than chasing short-term gains. We talked about the need to invest only in what you understand or can research sufficiently to make an informed decision. We also touched on the effects of inflation, taxes, and fees on your investment returns.

By now you understand that the choice and timing of an individual investment is only part of the puzzle. Here we build on the Principles of Investing already outlined, focusing on long-term investing before we dive deeper into the finer points of taxes, pensions, insurance, and infinite banking.

Focus on the Total Return on Your Investments

So far, when considering the rates of return on investments, we simplified our examples to consider the effects of a single consideration, be that inflation, interest rate, or method of calculation. You must consider all of these in conjunction with the effects of taxes, fees, and commissions that eat into your profits on any investment. Most headline figures and projections don't show the results of these, so you must do some digging around, ask some questions, and possibly create projections of your own.

If you haven't thought about stock fees and taxes, consider this before making a large investment: Set up an investment account that allows for previous and future tax entries on capital gains, income, and ultimately dividends. Although taxes and fees aren't the focus of any investment, it's smart to incorporate them when calculating long-term returns.

Don't Follow Popular Trends

If anyone tells you they can guarantee where the market will be a month, a year, or a decade from now, take your money and run the other way as fast as you can. Similarly, if anyone starts their investment pitch with anything along the lines of, "Everyone's getting into…," steer clear.

Despite the confidence of most pundits, *no one* knows what will happen or when. It's generally a good idea to avoid following the markets unless you do it via an index tracker. By the time your colleagues and friends start to invest in a sector, it's usually too late to secure a capital gain. By the time most traditional investors have heard of a new investment opportunity, the prices are driven too high and the investment itself is overpopulated, making it a poor financial choice for any investor seeking long-term value.

If you look through a few decades of investing in fads, you quickly realize there is most often a negative return on investment. Statistically, average investors who follow a hype or trend lose an average of 3.7% each year, compared to people who ignore trends.

Diversify and Stay Flexible

Remember, diversification refers to spreading your investment across multiple asset classes representing stocks, insurance, and real estate, rather than obsessing over holding stocks in multiple companies or properties. You can spread risk within an asset class you are unfamiliar with by using an index-linked mutual fund or by partnering with an expert in the field.

No matter how much you diversify your portfolio, you can never remove all forms of risk. Multiple frequent trades increase your costs and can swallow your profit, making over-diversification as big an issue as over-specialization.

Having a flexible investment strategy helps you find new and upcoming investment opportunities regardless of the market condition. Factors beyond the market's control – think economic collapse, manmade and natural disasters, and changes in legislation – can alter the financial landscape overnight. *Your ability to roll with the punches and adapt to a new situation serves you better in the long run than any amount of diversification.*

Calculated Risk Is Okay

We all want to avoid risk, while still achieving a high return on our investments. We also understand the correlation between risks and rewards. We expect high-risk investments to come with attendant high rewards if the investment pays off and accept that occasionally we lose out. We balance that risk with safer investments with lower rates and more predictable returns.

The trick is finding the balance. Too much risk and you end up losing money hand over fist or wiping out your entire portfolio. Not enough risk and your portfolio can't grow enough to cover taxes and inflation, much less provide an income or lump sum when you need it.

When considering any investment there are two types of risk:

- Systematic Risks: Situations that end up affecting the entire market (wars and market recessions)

- Unsystematic Risks: Risk that is specific to one company's stocks and securities.

Systemic risk can be mitigated by spreading your investment across multiple asset classes, even though it can't be avoided completely.

Minimize unsystematic risks by investing in an index-linked fund or by researching individual companies.

The point is that there is always some element of risk. The key is to make it "calculated" risk.

Learn from Previously Failed Investments

You can't eliminate risk, so understand that from time to time, investments don't pan out. No one has a clean investment history. Plenty of successful investors failed miserably in the past.

What's important is that when successful investors make a poor financial decision, they learn from their mistakes, whereas the unsuccessful investor sees only failure. No matter how large or small the loss, it's crucial to take a few steps back and look at the decisions that led to the loss. Note what went wrong, learn from it, and take steps to ensure you don't make the same mistake again.

One of the biggest reasons for failed investments is allowing emotional attachments, fear, or greed to interfere with the decision-making process. It's hard to ignore your impulses and learn how to discipline yourself when it comes to taking risks with large amounts of money, but if you allow your emotions to rule your portfolio, you descend into no better than gambling with your future.

Watch Your Investments Periodically

Investing isn't a set-it-and-forget-it game. Even with a long-term strategy, evaluate on a periodic basis the performance of each of your assets and make sure it still meets your criteria.

A day trader is glued to the screen all day, buying and selling when the market moves a few fractions of a percentage point. A stock trader uses trailing stop losses to lock in gains and minimize losses. The long-term investor doesn't follow the market as closely, but still needs to know how his investments are performing to stay on track.

If your investment strategy relies on regular dividends from your stocks, for example, and one of your holdings fails to pay them, evaluate cashing in and transferring your funds to an alternative vehicle. If your focus is on property development, when an asset moves out of development and into the operational phase, you want to sell it to free up cash to invest in a new development.

How closely and how frequently you monitor your assets depends on your personal strategy. Whatever it is, set a schedule for checking in and spend time assessing your portfolio.

Conclusion

There is no perfect investment strategy. Humans are notoriously optimistic when it comes to setting long-term goals. Market fluctuations, economic conditions, and occasional lapses in judgment all occur. Taxes, inflation, and fees inevitably eat into your returns. But with a realistic outlook and a healthy attitude toward risk, you can learn to separate your emotional response to setbacks from your decision making, thereby increasing your chances of reaching those goals

The first half of this book concentrated on developing an investor's mindset allowing you to increase your net worth over time. Now it's time to switch gears and think about how you protect the assets you accumulate.

We look at taxes and how you can pay less of them, insurance, pensions, and other forms of asset protection before we move on to consider how you can control the way your wealth is distributed during your lifetime and beyond. We investigate giving to charity responsibly, estate planning and the growing importance of family offices, along with a side trip to learn how to deal with sudden inheritance or any substantial, sudden increase in income or net worth.

Finally, we round out this primer on wealth preservation with suggestions for further reading, coupled with action steps you can take to put your newfound knowledge into practice. As always, you have an open invitation to join us at Financial wellnessMD.com to continue your journey.

The only difference between death and taxes is that death doesn't get worse every time Congress meets."

Will Rogers

Coming to Grips with Taxes

"I'm in the top income tax bracket and pay a fortune in taxes annually. I've heard about tax-efficient savings and investment, but I'm not sure what I can and can't do to keep more of my money from Uncle Sam. How can I stop taxes from gobbling up my profits?"

Benjamin Franklin famously said, "In this world, nothing can be said to be certain except death and taxes." Don't be fooled by the IRS's description of the tax system as a "voluntary" one. It's the kind of political doublespeak that would land a private advertising agency in hot water.

Make no mistake, despite what tax protesters like to believe, tax in the United States is <u>mandatory</u>. You don't get to opt in to be liable for it and you can never entirely opt out of paying it. You can't decide whether to pay or not pay, unless you're happy for the IRS to come and take your assets.

What you do have is a measure of control. You can use tax reduction strategies to minimize the taxes you pay. You can choose to make use of tax-efficient savings vehicles including pensions, life insurance, and reinvesting capital gains to defer tax to a later date. You can choose to submit your tax return based on your own calculations, rather than having the IRS calculate the taxes you owe based on what can be limited information.

You can't underreport your income and inflate your deductions without facing fines, interest charges on the taxes due, and possible imprisonment if you are audited and false reports come to light. That is tax evasion. Tax avoidance is not only legal, it's an important part of wealth building. Tax evasion is a criminal offense under *U.S. Code Title 26.*[14]

How to Reduce Your Taxable Income

There is no way to cover all the nuances of tax reduction in this book. I <u>can</u> offer you a simple three-step process to get you on the right track. You can find more detailed

---

[14] LII / Legal Information Institute,. 1982. "26 U.S. Code § 7201 - Attempt To Evade Or Defeat Tax".
https:/ www.law.cornell.edu/uscode/text/26/7201.

information about each of these steps at FinancialWellnessMD.com.

Make the Most of Tax Exemptions

Include only taxable income on your tax return. Non-taxable income includes:

- Child support
- Proceeds from life insurance policies
- Inheritances, which will already have been subject to inheritance tax
- Workers compensation payments or compensation awarded because of physical injury
- Education scholarships or grants
- Income paid to your 401k or IRA retirement account (within limits)
- If you're in a state that takes income tax, you can deduct either state and local income tax or state and local sales tax, but not both, so you need to work out which option gives you the larger deduction.

If you're married, figure out whether you are better off filing jointly or separately. Also, consider if it's better to take standard deductions for things like medical expenses and health insurance, mortgage interest, losses due to thefi or accident, and charitable contributions. You can use sofiware like TurboTax to help you calculate which options give the minimal tax liability.

Whether you use standard or itemized deductions, you can claim deductions for real estate taxes, loss because of a Federally Declared Disaster, and taxes on federally-sponsored programs including energy-efficient vehicles and appliance purchases, and home office expenses.

Set up an LLC

If you're employed and file a W-2 tax return, your employer deducts taxes for you and pays you a net salary. While some unreimbursed work-related expenses can be deductible under IRS Schedule A,[15] these deductions are limited to 2% of your adjusted net income. Deductible Employee Business expenses include:

- Business travel away from home
- Business use of your car
- Business meals and entertainment
- Travel
- Use of your home
- Education
- Supplies
- Tools
- Miscellaneous expenses

By setting up a Limited Liability Corporation (LLC) and filing a 1099 tax return as a self-employed individual, you can deduct a wider range of legitimate business expenses and avoid the 2% cutoff. If you set up a sideline consulting or public speaking business or a real-estate investment company – provided you document your spending and how it relates to your business – you can deduct:

- Use of home for business
- A portion of your phone and internet costs
- Health Insurance premiums
- 50% of the cost of meals when traveling or entertaining clients
- 50% of other business entertainment expenses
- The cost of travel longer than one day outside the city of your business's home address

---

[15] Irs.gov,. 2016. "Employee Business Expenses". https:/ www.irs.gov/uac/Employee-Business-Expenses-1.

- The business portion of car costs, either by mileage or as a proportion of actual costs
- Interest on business loans
- Magazine subscriptions and book purchases that relate to your business
- Education and continuing professional development course costs that relate to an existing business
- Contributions to self-employed retirement plans

Try to form a business, or even multiple businesses. If you spend a good amount of money on any one thing, set up another company. If you set up a rental company, and you look at rental property when you travel, your travel expenses become tax-deductible. Even if you're self-employed or own a practice, having an unrelated second business can allow you to deduct expenses in relation to one business that are disallowed in relation to the other.

Use Tax-Efficient Investment Vehicles

Once you maximize deductions, minimize your tax liability further by pumping as much as you can into tax-efficient savings and investment vehicles. The importance of choosing the right pension vehicle comes up in the next chapter. For now, let me simply tell you to max out your contributions. Other investment vehicles that allow you to shield your income from tax while also offering the potential to earn an income include:

- Tax exempt state and municipal bonds
- US Treasury Bonds
- Stocks (currently tax-capped at 15%)
- Investment real estate, which allows you to write off a portion of rental income
- Permanent insurance policies, which allow you to take a tax-free loan against the cash value of the policy.

Anytime you can invest in a vehicle that offers a lower tax rate instead of money that is otherwise liable for taxation at a higher rate, you retain the difference. If you must pay tax at 40% on $50,000 ($20,000 tax bill) but instead invest the money in an instrument taxed at 15%, that same cash is only liable for $7500 in tax. Even better, in most cases you can defer the tax until a later date and earn interest on it in the meantime!

"I had a pension that I was paying into for 27 years... It's now worth less than a Herman Cain endorsement."

Martin Bashir

Why You Need a Self-Directed Roth IRA

"I want to invest in rental real estate for my retirement, but my pension provider only allows me to invest in stocks and bonds. I've heard about self-directed IRAs, but I don't understand them. What are the benefits, and how do I set up one?"

In May 2015, the Government Accountability Office (GAO) released a report showing almost half of all Americans over the age of 55 have no retirement savings. Almost one-third of those have no Defined Benefit retirement plan or non-retirement savings to draw on, and many either don't own their own home or still have a mortgage.

To make matters worse, while many workers over 55 expect to retire later as well as work in their retirement, a survey of current retirees showed that half were forced to retire earlier than planned due to ill health, workplace restructuring, or changes in their personal circumstances. Another GAO report found that 3% of people over 65 are still paying off student loans, the majority in relation to their own educations and not those of their kids and grandkids.[16]

Unless you want to be one of those statistics and face poverty in retirement, or you believe that Social Security gives you enough to live on, you need to tackle retirement savings.

Traditional IRA - 401K

As far as I can see, the only reason to have a 401k is to take advantage of an employer's matching contributions. Ed Slott of IRAHelp.com says, "That is free money and you shouldn't leave any of it on the table."

If your employer isn't going to match your contributions, skip it and put your money in a Roth IRA instead.

The traditional reasoning for adopting a 401k retirement plan is to take advantage of the tax deductions on your contributions. The problem is that payouts from your 401k

---

[16] Jeszeck, Charles A. 2014. *OLDER AMERICANS Inability To Repay Student Loans May Affect Financial Security Of A Small %age Of Retirees*. Ebook. 1st ed. United States Government Accountability Office.
http:/ www.gao.gov/assets/670/665709.pdf.

afier retirement are taxable, and if you need to access them more than six months before your 60th birthday, you also face an early withdrawal penalty tax. If you opt to work longer and retire later, you can only contribute a maximum of six months afier you turn 70. Then required minimum distributions start.

On a well-managed fund, taxes on payouts are likely more in real terms than on contributions, regardless of current and future tax rates. As an example, if you pay $5000 into a 401K and are eligible for deductions, you might save
$2000 in tax on that contribution in the year it's made. If it sits in your retirement account for 30, and achieves a CAGR of 8%, it would generate $54,338. Even at a 10% tax rate, you are liable to pay $5433 in tax upon its disbursement. If you grow your 401K pension for 30 years, understand you grow the taxes that are due on that, too.

Also, if you're a higher earner, with adjusted Annual Gross Income (AGI) of more than $60,000 for a single taxpayer or more than $96,000 for a couple filing jointly, the tax-deductible benefits of contributions phase out and disappear altogether if you earn more than $70,000 as a single taxpayer or $116,000 as a couple. Deductions are also reduced if you or your spouse are covered by an employers Defined Benefit plan, even if you declined to participate or failed to make the minimum contributions in that plan.[17]

Another problem with 401Ks and Traditional IRAs is the institutions offering them restrict investment options to stocks, bonds, mutual funds, and CDs because of a perceived lack of investor sophistication. With a conventional IRA you have an account with a financial institution, and they invest the money on your behalf.

---

[17] Irs.gov,. 2016. "Publication 590-A (2015), Contributions To Individual Retirement Arrangements (Iras)".
https:/ www.irs.gov/publications/p590a/ch01.html#en_US _2014_publink1000230433.

While you can choose from their portfolio of stocks and bonds which investments on which you want to focus, the options available to you are limited to investments the institution can make a commission on.

If you want to invest in real estate, the bank can't make a commission on that, so not only do they not sell you these options, they write clauses into the contract that disallow this type of investment in your portfolio.

Roth IRA

Roth IRAs offer several benefits over a traditional IRA, despite contributions not being deductible.[18]

- While contributions are not tax-deductible, qualified distributions are not included in your income.

- You can contribute to a Roth IRA with adjusted AGI of up to $129,000 for a single person and $191,000 for a married couple filing jointly. You can still contribute to a Roth IRA even if you can't contribute to a 401K.

- While annual contributions are capped at $5500, you can make excess contributions, which are liable to a 6% excise tax.

- There is no age limit on contributions or enforced required minimum distributions, so you can leave your money in your retirement account until you need it.

- You can set up a self-directed Roth IRA, giving you access to a much wider range of investment opportunities like gold, real estate, venture capital, and even private loans.

---

[18] Irs.gov,. 2016. "Publication 590-A (2015), Contributions To Individual Retirement Arrangements (Iras)".
https:/ www.irs.gov/publications/p590a/ch02.html#en_US _2014_publink1000230988.

If you have a 401K and are disillusioned with its performance, you can convert your traditional IRA into a Roth IRA by way of a Roth Conversion through either a rollover or a trustee transfer. That means you can move funds from your current pension plan to a Roth IRA and pay the tax due on it now and avoid paying more later.

Self-Directed Roth IRAs

The biggest benefit to a self-directed Roth IRA is the ability to invest in high-yield investments. A self-directed IRA enables you to take control of your investment portfolio and build your retirement income by allowing you to include real estate, notes, private placements, tax lien certificates, and other types of assets.

When you set up a self-directed IRA, you effectively set up a trust to manage your assets on your behalf, and all assets included in the IRA must be owned, managed, and sold by that trust, with all proceeds going into it.

With a self-directed IRA, you are the trustee of your own trust and retain control over your own assets. Now THAT'S taking control of your finances.

There are rules about what you can and cannot include in a self-directed IRA, most notably self-dealing limitations. You can't sell your or your family's existing assets into it, for example. Nor can you stuff it with tangible assets of which you currently enjoy benefits, like artwork, antiques, various other collectibles, and life insurance policies. Furthermore, you cannot borrow from a self-directed IRA or use the assets in it as collateral.

Self-directed IRA investments are not guaranteed and as such, a self-directed IRA is not for everyone. They are designed to allow investors who understand what they are doing and accept the risks to determine their own portfolio.

Currently, only an estimated 2% of all pensions are self-directed Roth IRAs. If even just half the American population have pension plans, that means 99% of people in the United States can't build a retirement portfolio using real estate or other alternative collateralized investments. The ability to leverage investment dollars and shelter the returns from the IRS in terms of retirement savings is beyond all but about 1% of the population.

Most people don't do so because the institutions that serve as custodians for their IRAs can't make commissions on assets in a self-directed IRA. In other words, since financial advisors receive a percentage of all assets under management, as well as fees from stock securities, it is not in their self-interest to allow you to manage or control your retirement funds. Other folks don't take advantage of self-directed IRAs because they imagine it's more complicated than it is.

Sometimes it's referred to as the checkbook IRA. The only thing that's different is that you control what you invest in. I put my money into a bank account for my IRA and when I find an investment I want to buy, I write a check from that account and buy the assets under my IRA account name. Then when I sell the asset, I get my money back and put it back into my IRA account. I can buy a note on a property, I can buy into a business, or I can make a money loan. It's simple.

How to Self-Direct Your Roth IRA

- Identify a self-directed Roth IRA provider and open an account. (You can find a list of providers at FinancialWellnessMD.com)
- Fund the account with your contributions or by a Roth Rollover.

- Research and identify suitable investments and use your IRA account checkbook to purchase them in the name of your IRA account.
- Manage the investment, ensuring all income generated is paid back into your Roth IRA account, and all expenses relating to it are drawn from that account. Remember, your IRA is effectively a separate entity and you must treat it that way.
- If you decide to sell the investment, proceeds from the sale are returned to the IRA account, tax free, and become available for reinvestment.

Several experts suggest that the decision to opt for a Traditional IRA or a Roth IRA depends on whether you plan to reinvest any savings on tax-deductible contributions, but I disagree. If you're going to spend them, you're better off in your retirement with a Roth IRA. If you expect to retire with income in a higher tax bracket than your current one, a Roth IRA is the way to go. In fact, even if you expect to retire in a lower tax bracket, you're better off with a Roth IRA.

Even though you can get a Self-Directed Traditional IRA and defer the tax on your contributions, it doesn't make financial sense. The whole point of a self-directed IRA is to take advantage of higher-yield investments. Therefore, in the long run, sheltering distributions is more important than claiming deductions. With the traditional method, we end up funding the government's retirement, not our own.

Three Steps to Self-Direct Your IRA

Step One — Choose an IRA provider

Step Two — Fund a Self-Directed IRA account

Step Three — Write a check from your S-D IRA account into your high yield investment vehicle

"Insurance - an ingenious modern game of chance in which the player is permitted to enjoy the comfortable conviction that he is beating the man who keeps the table."

Ambrose Bierce

Asset Protection: When Insurance Plays a Vital Role

Chad Armstrong

"I know I need insurance, but the cost of premiums seems astronomical. There are so many different types; I get lost in the definitions. What types of insurance do I really need?"

Insurance plays an important role in financial planning. Personal insurance falls into three main camps; life, disability, and long-term care. Each of these has a role in protecting your assets during all stages of accumulation.

Life Insurance

Life insurance policies protect your loved ones in the event of death. You can insure against the loss of future income of a breadwinner; provide protection for a partnership buyout; protect a business against the loss of a key employee; plan for estate liquidity needs; and provide asset protection from creditors.

In almost every scenario, the death benefit is tax free. Life insurance is sold as either term or permanent cover, although some permanent insurance can act more like term.

Term Insurance

Term insurance is the least expensive type of life insurance, often recommended due to the low cost. There are several types of term policies on the market:

- Level Term Insurance pays out a fixed lump sum and usually offers fixed premiums over the length of the term.
  - Increasing Term Insurance pays out more in later years, allowing for the cost of inflation, but premiums will also rise over the term.
  - Decreasing Term Insurance pays out less in later years, making it an ideal cover for repayment mortgages. Because the coverage decreases over time, premiums are lower than level term insurance.
  - Renewable Term Insurance gives the policyholder the right to renew at the end of the term, provided premiums are paid on time every time. Although

premiums may increase at the renewal date, coverage isn't affected by health issues not present at the original time of purchase. Premiums are initially higher for someone who is diagnosed with a serious condition and becomes otherwise uninsurable, even escalating premiums provide peace of mind and death benefits that might otherwise be unobtainable.

Because a longer term means the insurance company is "on the hook" for a prolonged period, premiums to cover the same amount over 30 years will be higher than the same cover over 10 or 20 years. However, unless the time coverage is needed can be predicted with accuracy beforehand (as in the case of mortgage repayment or key-personnel coverage), it's usually better to opt for the longest term available. You can never predict when something might happen that will make it harder or more expensive to get coverage, but won't trigger a payout, such as chronic illness.

Permanent Life Insurance

Whereas term insurance policies pay out on death within a certain period, permanent life insurance policies are built to pay a death benefit when you die, regardless of when that is.

The main types of permanent policies are Whole Life, Universal Life, Variable Universal Life, Guaranteed Universal, and the more recent Equity Indexed Universal Life insurance. Premiums are higher for permanent life policies, because a payout is inevitable, but your premiums are split between purchasing life coverage, and investing for future growth. Investment returns are credited to your policy account and accumulate. This means your policy has a cash-in value that grows over time.

Most states allow some credit protection of cash values, with states like Texas allowing full protection. Better still, cash values grow tax-deferred under the law and can be used during your lifetime through a return of premium (tax free) and if necessary, policy loans (tax free) with a tax-free benefit at the death of the insured.

Pretty good planning opportunities abound with the right type of policy and funding of that policy, especially when you can control the timing of when you pull those funds out of the policy, such as to supplement income when capital markets are down so that you don't have to take permanent losses from your pension.

- Whole Life is the basic permanent life insurance and offers the features described above.

- Universal Life provides the ability to skip premium payments. This is a nice feature when times are bad, but without proper maintenance the policies become a very expensive term policy. They can run out of steam (cash to support the death benefit) in later years when it is needed most.

- Variable Universal Life policy cash values are invested in a portfolio with an asset allocation of the client's choosing, based on their investment policy statement (IPS). These policies have the same basic characteristics as a regular Universal Life policy, with the exception that the cash is in the market and not invested in the carrier's own investment portfolio as Whole life and Universal Life are.

- Guaranteed Universal Life policies are built around estate tax liquidity, with no cash buildup. They can be used as "term for life" policies, but please keep in mind there is no cash value, and premiums must be made on time every time or you risk losing your "guarantee," without which the policy lapses.

- Equity Indexed Universal Life. Until changes are made to the flexibility that the insurance carriers have, I advise staying away. With an Equity Index Linked Insurance policy, the investment returns are tied to an index market, but with a "cap rate" and a "floor rate," designed to even out the effects of bad years by withholding and reinvesting the surplus in good years. So, if your policy is capped at 12% and the market performs at 15%, you are credited with 12% and the 3% difference is reinvested. If, however, the market loses, you are credited with the floor rate, which may be 2%, guaranteeing a minimum level of growth. Unfortunately, floor rates are ofien set at zero, while the insurance company retains the right to lower the cap rate, limiting the benefits to the point where the policy may be better for the insurance company than it is for you. Stick to whole life, universal life, or variable universal.

Disability Insurance

If, like most people, you rely on an earned income, this is the most important insurance coverage you can have. Imagine a situation where you are unable to earn a living, your health costs just went up and the expenses remain, all before you saved enough to retire. Disability Insurance protects against such a loss.

The problem is that you can never buy as much insurance as you need. When people ask, "How much should I get?" there is only one answer:

"As much as the insurance company will sell you."

Some people forgo disability insurance, thinking they can just cut back on expenses – to which I say go ahead and try it. Cut back now. Live on 50% and save the rest. And good luck with that course of action!

When considering disability insurance, there are a few points to consider:

- Foremost is the financial strength of the insurance company. The weaker the company, the more likely they are to question a claim. Look for a company with strong financial ratings from Standard & Poor's,

Moody's, Fitch, or A.M. Best for the best chance of a payout.

- Define disability. Look for an own-occupation definition. You want a policy that pays out if you can't do your job, not one that refuses to pay out on the grounds you could take a lower paying job or work in another industry.
- Maximize your individual policy. Although individual policy premiums are higher than group policies, individual policies are much stronger contracts than Group Disability policies.

For physicians who operate in a small practice, there is also a disability policy called Disability Overhead Expense (DOE). This reimburses business expenses, so in the event you become disabled and have people who rely on you (staff, patients, partners, etc.), it allows you to maintain the practice until you can either sell it or recover and return to work (for example, if you end up having orthopedic surgery and cannot use your hands for 90 days). The premiums for DOE are a deductible expense, since the benefits are used for tax-deductible expenses and is beneficial to any healthcare provider who performs procedures as part of the job.

Ofien when reviewing partnership agreements that contain buy/sell provisions, disabilities are mentioned as a trigger for the buy/sell clause. Rarely is a funding vehicle in place, such as Disability Buyout insurance. Following a waiting period of anywhere from 30 to 365 days to allow for the sale of the practice/business, these policies pay a lump sum or a stream of installments. Therefore, should one partner become disabled, then afier a predetermined period the partnership agreement triggers a sale to the other partner(s).

Long-Term Care Insurance

The purpose of a long-term care (LTC) policy is to provide funds in case the insured suffers an inability to carry out any two activities of daily living. These include continence, bathing, transferring, dressing and eating, as well as cognitive functions.

More than half our population will need qualifying medical care during their lifetimes and the cost of this care is enormous. Many people mistakenly think that Medicare or their health insurance policies takes care of this.

Having an LTC policy in force allows you to plan with more certainty. You don't have to cordon off money because you might need long term care 20 or 30 years from now. You don't have to worry whether you (or your partner afier your death) will receive the care you need or be able to stay in your own home instead of moving to a facility. A good LTC insurance policy allows you to stay in your own home as long as possible.

Although the tax implications are beyond the scope of this book, LTC premiums may be tax deductible and can be paid in tax-free exchanges from annuities and life insurance.

The downside to LTC, disability, and term insurance is that if you don't file a claim you lose all your premiums. Their real value is in piece of mind, and in being able to use available funds as you see fit throughout the term.

Mutual vs. Stock

Another consideration is whether a company is stock-owned or a mutual company. Stock-owned companies are publicly traded businesses owned by the shareholders. They trade on an exchange and their interests are more closely aligned with increased shareholder value.

Mutual insurance companies are not traded. They are privately owned by their policyholders, who are the shareholders. This relationship creates a natural alignment of interests between the policyholders and the company.

Amir Says

Whew! Thanks, Chad, for the insurance roundup. It's a huge subject and we can't hope to cover everything in a short financial primer. If you want to learn more, visit the resources section of FinancialWellnessMD.com, where my team and I have gathered a lot more information for you.

I want to reiterate Chad's point on disability insurance. Too many doctors, confronted every day with the devastating effects of ill health, continue to bury their heads and think it won't happen to them.

Take a long look at your budget. How many of your outgoings can you realistically reduce or eliminate if your income is cut off? Would you have to sell your home and downsize? Do you have enough money in the bank to keep you afloat? Would you be happy to take a low-paying job, or work in another sector? No? You need an own-occupation disability insurance policy.

*"Until Americans feel that their core asset - their homes - are stabilized, they are not going to **have the animal spirits**, and they will continue to have less buying power."*

Kevin O'Leary

Asset Protection

"I have own-occupation disability insurance, life insurance, and long-term care insurance. Other than insurance, how can I protect my assets?"

Asset protection is utilized to keep assets out of creditors' hands in the event of financial difficulty. It also plays an integral role in estate planning and limiting tax liability. It's advisable to set up asset protection plans well before they are needed, as they are much harder and ofien impossible to implement when a crisis already occurred.

Foreign Asset Protection Trusts (FAPTs)

The ultimate in asset protection would be an offshore trust in the Cook Islands. With these trusts, before funds are released everyone in the trust must agree it is in the best interests of the beneficiary to withdraw those funds. Since you are the beneficiary of the trust, your custodians are hardly likely to agree that release of assets to creditors is in your best interests. Also, because these trusts are held outside U.S. jurisdiction, assets held in them are ofien outside the reach of U.S. courts. However, where assets are located domestically, creditors can still enforce a judgment.[19]

Domestic Asset Protection Trusts

Domestic Asset Protection Trusts (DAPT) set up on behalf of someone else to protect assets held in the trust from the beneficiaries' creditors aren't new. Until recently, however, it wasn't possible to set up a trust and name yourself as a beneficiary to gain the same protection. There are currently fourteen states which allow DAPTs, with Nevada being the most popular.[20]

---

[19] Lighthouse-trust.com,. 2016. "The Early Demise Of The Domestic Asset Protection Trust | Lighthouse Trust".
http:/ lighthouse-trust.com/news/the-early-demise-of-the-domestic-asset-protection-trust/.

[20] Oshins, Steve. 2015. *6Th Annual Domestic Asset Protection Trust State Rankings Chart*. Ebook. 1st ed. in Las Vegas,

With a DAPT, the custodians must agree to the release of funds and will only release assets if everyone in the trust agrees to it. By law, your custodians are only required to release assets if ascertained that to do so benefits you, including moving assets to another trust.

You don't have to live in the state or hold assets within the state to set up an asset protection trust. For example, you can buy real estate in Dallas and hold it within a DAPT in Nevada.

The validity of DAPTs has come under some attack through the U.S. courts. In 2013, an Alaska DAPT was deemed invalid and unenforceable in *Waldron v Huber*.

The strength of a DAPT rests in the settlor's ability to select the applicable law for the trust, provided this isn't in violation of "a strong public policy of the state with which, as to the matter at issue, the trust has its most significant relationship." If most of your assets are held outside the DAPT elective state with only a token deposit in the DAPT state, not only could the courts disregard the trust but transfers into the trust could be regarded as fraudulent if they are deemed to be made specifically with the intent to evade, hinder, or defeat a creditor.

Both foreign and domestic asset protection trusts are useful in managing the transfer of assets between beneficiaries and for limiting tax liability. It is important to note that trusts must be drawn up with care by an expert. A lapse in judgment can lead to an increase in tax liability, rather than shield the settlor's estate from it.[21]

Nevada: Law Offices of Oshins & Associates. http:/ www.oshins.com/images/DAPT_Rankings.pdf.

[21]Rothschild, Gideon, and Daniel S. Rubin. 2002. *Self-Settled Asset Protection Trusts*. Ebook. 1st ed. New York: Moses & Singer LLP. http:/ www.mosessinger.com/site/files/Self-Settled%20Asset%20Protection%20Trusts.pdf.

Family Limited Partnerships

In the chapter, "Coming to Grips with Taxes," I suggested setting up a Limited Liability Corporation (LLC) to take advantage of self-employment tax breaks. Another way to handle this and help shield your assets from inheritance tax or gifi tax is to set up a Family Limited Partnership (FLP). Both LLCs and Limited Partnerships provide a level of personal protection against creditors in the event of financial difficulty because the creditor must sue the company and not you directly.

With a family limited partnership, you can hold assets jointly with your family. If properly set up and managed, this can help limit an estate's exposure to inheritance tax by transferring asset ownership during one partner's lifetime to other partners.

There must be a legitimate business element in the formation of the partnership, however, and not just the desire to limit inheritance and gifi tax liability. Such business elements include creating a formal decision-making process and avoidance of complicated co-tenancies; utilizing professional financial management services for a family portfolio; and centralizing management of the family assets.[22]

Pensions and Inheritance

Finally, it's worth mentioning that pensions are also exempt under ERISA (Employee Retirement Income Security Act of 1974). Pensions can be bequeathed in your will, but the treatment of them depends on who inherits

---

[22] fizerbeck,. 2016. "Family Limited Partnerships In Estate Planning". http:/ www.fizerbeck.com/family-limited-partnerships-in-estate-planning.

them and whether you have started withdrawing from the pension at your time of death. [23]

Children who inherit an IRA may take distributions over their lifetime or be forced to take benefits over the course of five years, according to how quickly they act. A spouse who inherits a Roth IRA may delay disbursements indefinitely or roll the pension over into her own account and name her own beneficiary, thereby keeping the pension fund out of the taxman's hands indefinitely.

Tax laws and inherited pensions are a complex subject we can't begin to fully cover in this book, but you can find out more at *FinancialWellnessMD.com*.

In general, Roth IRAs – where taxes were paid on contributions, thereby making payouts tax-exempt – put more money in the hands of your loved ones and less in the hands of the IRS.

---

[23] Steiner, Sheyna. 2016. "8 Ways To Go Wrong With An Inherited IRA | Bankrate.Com". *Bankrate.Com*.
http:/ www.bankrate.com/finance/retirement/ways-to-go-wrong-with-inherited-ira-1.aspx.

"The Infinite Banking Concept is not a bank; it is a thought process that represents a major paradigm shift."

Nelson Nash

Infinite Banking and the Rich Man's Roth IRA

"I've heard about infinite banking and some say it's a way to use insurance to pay for life's major purchases, while others say it's a way to pay less tax. It all seems very complicated. What is infinite banking about and can it work for me?"

In most cases, you buy as much life insurance as you can afford because you want as much money as possible to go to your family when you die. With Infinite Banking, it's different.

Remember we talked about the benefits of Roth IRAs, where you pay the tax on the money you put in rather than on the money you take out? We also briefly touched on the limitations of Roth IRAs in terms of contributions for high earners. So how do you build a pension fund if you can't contribute to an IRA?

You use a permanent life insurance policy colloquially known as "the rich man's Roth IRA."

In most cases, you buy as much life insurance as you can afford because you want as much money as possible to go to your family when you die.

With Infinite Banking, it's different. You buy a token amount of life insurance, say $1 million. Instead of paying the premiums, you put your money into an associated account. That way you get a large amount of money in your life insurance policy. When it matures when you are 65 you get it tax-free because it's funded with afier-tax dollars. In the meantime, the money is invested in equities and can earn anywhere from 4 - 8% for you.

What if you later decide you want to invest in something or make a business loan? If you're lending to a family member, that is not allowed under the self-dealing rules of a Roth IRA. So instead of taking out a bank loan and paying retail interest rates, you can take a loan against your whole life insurance policy and pay a lower rate of interest on that. Then you can lend it out at a higher rate than you are paying and bank the difference. It's a kind of arbitrage, or lending on the margins.

Let's say you have $100,000 cash value in your whole life policy, earning 8%. You want to invest $20,000 in a rental real estate property that gives you a 15% internal rate of return. Remember, the internal RoR has already factored in your mortgage and other related costs, so that 15% is your profit. If you withdraw the $20,000 from your insurance policy and invest it in the real estate deal, you earn 8% on $80,000 ($6400) and 15% on $20,000 ($3000).

But that's not how whole-life insurance works. Instead of withdrawing the money, you take out a loan against it at favorable interest rates compared to commercial lending, with no restrictions on its use. It's also tax-free since you've already paid the premiums and funded the account with post-tax dollars.

So, you take out a loan of $20,000 against your life policy at 4% interest. You still have the $100,000 earning 8% ($8000). The insurance company lends you the $20,000 using your insurance policy as collateral and you earn 15% on the $20,000. You make $3000 on the $20,000 and pay out $800 of that in interest.

Now, instead of making $9400, you make $10,200 on the same deal. You have the choice of reinvesting the money in another deal with high interest yields and just paying the interest or paying it back into your policy.

As with everything, there are potential downsides. Whole life insurance policies are not eligible for loans until afier a predetermined time, which is as much as ten years. Make sure your policy is set up to use the cash value to pay minimum premiums in case of financial difficulty. If you miss premiums, you could lose coverage completely or your policy converted into a paid-up policy with reduced benefits.

If you fail to repay an amount borrowed against your life insurance policy cash value, it's deducted from the cash value of the policy, reducing the amount available for future borrowing. If you die with a policy loan outstanding, it's deducted from the face value of the policy, leaving your beneficiaries with less than expected.

R. Nelson Nash further elevates this principle of taking a loan against the cash value of a whole-of-life insurance policy with his Infinite Banking concept. On infinitebanking.org, he argues that "your need for finance, during your lifetime, is much greater than your need for protection."

The purpose of Infinite Banking, he says, is to "recapture the interest that one is paying to banks and finance companies for the major items that we need during a lifetime, such as automobiles, major appliances, education, homes, investment opportunities, business equipment, etc." Infinite Banking, then, is not just about investment, but about using financial arbitrage to fund your lifestyle. It does require long-term thinking and the discipline to replenish funds in your policy account, so you don't wipe it out with unpaid interest.

"Making money is easy. It is. The difficult thing in life is not making it; it's keeping it."

John McAfee

Wealth Preservation and the Sudden Wealth Syndrome

Carlos Padial III, CFP®

Author and Financial Planner

ConsciousMillionaire.com

"I'm about to sell my practice and take a part-time position as a stepping stone to retirement. I'll get a healthy check for it and I don't want to squander it. I want to make sure there's enough to last me for years to come. What's the best thing for me to do?"

Most people can't fathom – and never experience – sudden wealth. For the few who do, whether through inheritance, acting, sports or even the lottery, without expert counseling and guidance, an unexpected windfall can become more a curse than a blessing.

Sudden Wealth Syndrome is a term coined by psychologist Steven Goldbart to describe issues that often accompany a giant financial windfall:

- Unexplained stress
- Feeling isolated from former friends
- Guilt over good fortune
- Extreme fear of losing newfound wealth
- Confusion and conflicting emotions

Except in the case of inheritance (and sometimes even then) sudden wealth comes unexpectedly. The beneficiary often has no training or experience to deal with the different set of problems financial abundance poses to their prior experience. Cautionary tales abound.

- MC Hammer, despite earning over $33 million in 1991, filed for bankruptcy in 1996.
- Dennis Rodman earned more than $29 million in salary throughout his basketball career, yet in 2012 owed an ex-wife $800,000+ in child support and currently has an estimated net worth of <u>negative</u> $1 million.
- Vin Baker blew the $97.4 million he earned during his 14-year career and was last reported working as a barista for Starbucks.
- Andrew "Jack" Whittaker thought he could handle his 2002 $315 million Powerball Jackpot since he was already worth $17 million, thanks to his construction company. After giving much of his fortune to charity, family, and friends, though, he was plagued by personal problems. He was the victim of several large-scale

thefis, lost family members to drugs and took to alcohol and gambling himself. He first claimed poverty in 2007 and recently faced charges of bouncing checks for $1.5 million in gambling debts.

Even those who worked to build a company and managed large sums of money for many years can fall victim to Sudden Wealth Syndrome upon the sale of those businesses. Nebraskan party favor mogul Terrence Watanabe built his father's Oriental Trading Co. into an empire that generated over $300 million in revenue when he sold it in 2000 for an undisclosed amount. Afier declaring his intention to devote his time to philanthropic interests, he soon became restless. In 2007, he blew $127 million gambling in Las Vegas, and in 2009 faced four felony charges for intent to defraud Caesar's Palace and Rio Casinos of $14.7 million.

Let's look at some steps to help you if you come into a windfall.

Take a Timeout First

No one wants to hear that they need to save their money when they just acquired millions of dollars. There are unique financial, tax, and emotional issues that, if not addressed properly, can cause the money to disappear almost as quickly as it came. It is important to take things slowly. Park your money into a short-term savings instrument or money market account while you clear your head.

Most of us are used to gradual money from earned income and building a nest egg over time. As our net worth increases, we adapt and become more financially sophisticated. Then there's the shock of sudden wealth. It's like being on the ground floor of a 70-story building and in mere seconds rocketing to the penthouse.

Assemble Your Team of Professionals

The first step is to find a trusted advisor and possibly a therapist. You need a team to guide you through the financial planning process and help you avoid common psychological and financial pitfalls.

You need advisors you can rely on and trust to assist you in taxes, accounting, investments, and law. Do background checks on your professional team using the State Bar Association (attorneys); State Board of Accountancy (CPAs); Financial Industry Regulatory Authority (FINRA); the Securities and Exchange Commission (SEC) (investments); and the Certified Financials Professionals Board (CFP®'s).

While you are in uncharted waters, you want to create a financial team composed of people who live and breathe in these waters.

Beware of "The Posse"

New wealth may attract new friends and estranged family members who pop up out of nowhere. A good rule of thumb is if they weren't around before you had money, they are less likely to stick around if you lose it.

Get a Comprehensive Financial Plan

Don't buy, invest or make any money decisions until you meet with a Certified Financial Planner™ and get an up-to-date Comprehensive Financial Plan. Create a budget even though it sounds silly if you've come into millions. Without a fixed spending plan, you can wake up one morning to discover your wealth is all gone.

Create a Wishlist

Brainstorm about all the things you want to do with the money. Don't hold back! Categorize each item as "want" or "if possible." "Want" items are important to you like a new home, paying for children's education, and donating to charity. "If possible" items are everything else: travel, gifts to family members, and quitting your job. Determine what's possible before you buy a house or car and before you quit your job. Determine how far your sudden money allows you to go. Give your wish list to your accountant or investment advisor to help you understand what you can do without getting into financial trouble down the road.

Get a Financial Education

You don't have to go back to school but do take time to get a financial education. Your financial team can explain concepts and strategies, so you understand them, though there's no substitute for studying these issues on your own.

Monitor Your Finances

Meet with your financial planner and/or CPA at least once a quarter. Make sure your entire financial team is on the same page. This means having all the members of the team come together to discuss your financial plan.

Diversify Your Wealth

There are many asset classes you have access to including stocks; bonds; ETFs; Mutual Funds; variable and fixed annuities; adaptive and tactical money managers; consumer/institutional/industrial real estate; oil and gas drilling programs; equipment leasing trusts; collateralized notes; hedge funds; coins; precious metals; CDs; life insurance; and of course, cash. If your financial professional doesn't offer these non-correlating asset classes, go with another advisor. The goal is to protect your sudden wealth, so it can turn into lasting wealth.

Create a Pension

A defined benefit pension allows you to shield a large sum of money from taxes. A married 45-year-old can shelter up to $320,000, while a married 55-year-old can protect up to $530,000.

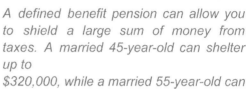

> A defined benefit pension can allow you to shield a large sum of money from taxes. A married 45-year-old can shelter up to
> $320,000, while a married 55-year-old can protect up to $530,000.

Amir Says

Thanks, Carlos, for highlighting the potential pitfalls of sudden wealth acquisition. It's interesting to note the kinds of investments that are available with high cash liquidity, where the barriers to entry are too high for most small or independent investors.

I think the major lesson to learn from this is that in many ways, it's better to build up your portfolio and learn about new investment classes as you can consider them, rather than exposing yourself to so many new opportunities all at once without the experience to evaluate them. And if you are "lucky" enough to find yourself in possession of a large fortune, it's important to take the time to weigh your decisions and know who to trust, to avoid being scammed.

"A rich man without charity is a rogue, and perhaps it would be no difficult matter to prove that he is also a fool."

Henry Fielding

Making the Most of Charity

"I want to give to good causes, and I want to make the most of my donations. What are the tax breaks for giving to charity?"

Emanuel Swedenborg, Swedish theologian, philosopher, and scientist argues that, "True charity is the desire to be useful to others with no thought of recompense."

In its purest form, charity is altruism in action. It isn't just giving money to corporations that meet a set of government criteria, it's giving your time, your energy, and sometimes your possessions to people who need them more than you. True charity doesn't look for a reward or recognition of any kind.

Multiple studies show that giving is as good for the donor as the recipient. Before we look at the financial aspects of charity, let's consider its less obvious benefits.

Giving Makes You Happy

In a 2008 study, *Feeling Good about Giving: The Benefits (and Costs) of Self-Interested Charitable Behavior*[24], Harvard Business School researchers found that "happier people give more, that giving indeed causes increased happiness, and that these two relationships may operate in a circular fashion." In the study, participants reported higher levels of satisfaction in spending money on others than spending on themselves, despite predicting the reverse result.

Giving is Good for Your Health

In *"Volunteerism and Mortality among the Community Dwelling Elderly,"* a paper published in the *Journal of Health Psychology*

---

[24] Anik, Lalin, Lara B. Aknin, Michael I. Norton, and Elizabeth W. Dunn. 2009. *Feeling Good About Giving: The Benefits (And Costs) Of Self-Interested Charitable Behavior Working Paper 10-012*. Ebook. 1st ed. Harvard Business School.
http:/ www.hbs.edu/faculty/Publication%20Files/10-012.pd

in 1999[25], Doug Oman reported the benefits of volunteering in older people. The study showed that volunteering for two or more organizations during a five-year period reduced the participant's risk of mortality by 44% afier controlling for other factors. Later similar studies, such as that by Stephanie Brown in 2003[26], showed that exhibiting caregiving behaviors conferred similar benefits.

Giving Creates Community Ties

You might think that when you give to charity, you get a temporary warm glow and that's it. You think the recipient of your gifi feels gratitude, feels more connected to you, and is more likely to support you in future. All of which is true mostly.

You might be surprised that the act of giving fosters feelings of community and closeness not just in the recipient, but in the donor too. When you donate, whether it's your time or your money, you become vested in the outcome. You align yourself with the needs of others and connect with them. You become part of something bigger than yourself.

---

[25] Oman, D., C. E. Thoresen, and K. Mcmahon. 1999. "Volunteerism And Mortality Among The Community-Dwelling Elderly". *Journal Of Health Psychology* 4 (3): 301-316. doi:10.1177/135910539900400301.

[26] Brown, Stephanie L., et al. 2009. *Caregiving Behavior Is Associated With Decreased Mortality Risk* . Ebook. 1st ed.
Association for Psychological Science.
http:/ www.rcgd.isr.umich.edu/news/Brown.Psych%20Science.May%2009.pdf.

Donations Are Tax Deductible

 Provided you donate to a charity that meets the tax-exempt non-profit criteria of section 501(c)(3) of the tax code, you can deduct the donation and associated costs from your income and reduce your tax bill. You can also deduct the cash value of assets or possessions."

Understanding the Deductible Value of Your Donations

If you receive goods in return for your donation, you must deduct the cash value of those goods from the donation. For example, if you attend a charity dinner and pay $500 a plate that normally costs you $100, you can only deduct
$400.

If you donate goods, such as golfing equipment to be awarded as a prize in a charity tournament, you can deduct the value of the goods. If you donate secondhand or antique items, get a fair market value appraisal of the items and document this.

You can also maximize the financial benefits of charitable donations by giving away assets you have owned for more than one year that have appreciated in value. That way, you can deduct the fair market value of the asset, while avoiding paying capital gains tax on the difference between purchase and disposal price.

When donating you plan to deduct from your income, make sure you get a receipt for it. The receipt needs to show the date, amount, and beneficiary of the donation, in case you are ever audited by the IRS.

You Cannot Deduct the Value of Your Time

While monetary donations to charities are tax-deductible, you cannot deduct the value of your time or other intangible items. Don't let that stop you from volunteering, though. The act of helping others has more than tax benefits. Also, you can deduct unreimbursed costs incurred in providing a service. If you traveled to speak at that charity dinner, for instance, if you paid the expenses out-of-pocket and the charity did not reimburse you for them, you could deduct those costs.

"It is always wise to look ahead, but difficult to look further than you can see."

Winston Churchill

Estate Planning During Your Lifetime

"I'm in my forties and in good health. I know I need to think about making a will, but I'm also concerned about what could happen to me during my lifetime. I've seen so many families ripped apart by difficult decisions when a loved one is incapacitated. How can I make sure that doesn't happen to my family?"

Most people think of estate planning in terms of making a will to ensure their assets are distributed according to their wishes at the end of their life. It's your written record of what you want to happen to your belongings when you pass away, as well as your preferences for healthcare and end-of-life care.

It is a common misconception that estate planning is for retired people only. The truth is, it's never too early to think about how you want your assets distributed, or who you want making the big decisions about your healthcare if you're unable to make them yourself.

According to *Forbes* magazine, approximately 50% of Americans have an estate plan in place. But that figure includes everyone with a will, medical, or financial directive. Estimates for those who have a living will range from 10 - 25%, with that figure rising to 38% when including those with a durable power of attorney.

Doctors and lawyers are no more likely to have these important documents in place than the general population. The very people who see firsthand the devastating effects of deterioration of health or loss of mental faculties are just as likely to procrastinate as anyone else.

Let's face it, none of us wants to talk about life-threatening illness, accidents, or old age, let alone death. That is, until something happens to someone around us that forces us into a reality check. A dear friend recently experienced her 88-year-old parents being diagnosed with "diminished capacity" by their gerontologist and neurologist. Both parents – six days apart in age – both diagnosed with dementia. Then came the questions:

- What kind of assets do they have?
- Do they have an estate plan in place?
- What if they need memory care?
- Who will pay for care and how long is it needed?
- Where do we find the time to take care of our own house and their home too?
- How can my practice survive managing my parents?
- What if this happens to my domestic partner or me?

Make a Living Will

Occasional cases like that of Terri Schiavo's family warring over her end-of-life care[27] make national headlines. Problems arise when parents, siblings, spouses, and children disagree over the assumed wishes of patients unable to speak for themselves. If you don't want your family to face the same heartbreaking schisms in the event of catastrophic illness, consider making a Living Will and encourage your loved ones to do the same.

A living will isn't about what happens afier you die, it's a document that explains what medical care you wish to receive if you are incapacitated. It details your wishes for life-prolonging medical treatment or lack thereof. Everyone has a personal and moral take of their own when it comes to end-of-life care. If you want to make the decision yourself, you must state it in your living will. This determines the course of treatment when it comes to unsettling decisions about terminal illness and unconsciousness, and it is legally binding for your doctors and physicians.

One of the reasons so few people have a living will, according to Peter Ditto, PhD, professor of psychology and social behavior at the University of California, Irvine, is that few of us want to micromanage our own death and prefer our loved ones to have at least some say in the matter.[28]

---

[27] Sanburn, Josh. 2015. "How Terri Schiavo Shaped The Right-To-Die Movement". *TIME.Com*. http:/ time.com/3763521/terri-schiavo-right-to-die-brittany-maynard/.

[28] American Psychological Association,. 2016. "The Living Will Needs Resuscitation". http:/ www.apa.org/monitor/2010/10/living-will.aspx

Another issue, he says, is that many of us change from one year to the next our opinions on how we want to be treated in a given situation, without being aware of the change. In a three-year study, Ditto and his associates found that when asked their preferences in three situations – one with mental but not physical impairment, one with physical but not mental impairment, and one with both and no chance of recovery – "only about 60% of participants expressed the same preferences all three years. In a follow-up study, they found that when participants did change their minds about a treatment, most didn't realize it, assuming that their past decisions were the same as their current ones." [29]

If you do make a living will, keep a copy and review it periodically to ensure it reflects your current views and not what you may have thought in the past. Also, make sure it conforms to state laws and review it if you move from one state to another, as it could become invalid.

If you're one of the many who want loved ones to be able to make decisions for you, consider designating a specific person whom you trust to make the best decisions and formalize this with a power of attorney.

Create a Power of Attorney

There are four types of powers of attorney, each giving powers to your attorney-in-fact to act as your agent and make decisions on your behalf.

- Limited Power of Attorney assigns the power to act on your behalf in specific circumstances, such as signing paperwork on your behalf when you are unavailable to do so. The circumstances granting power of attorney

---

[29] Oman, D., C. E. Thoresen, and K. Mcmahon. 1999. "Volunteerism And Mortality Among The Community-Dwelling Elderly". *Journal Of Health Psychology* 4 (3): 301-316. doi:10.1177/135910539900400301.

and time when they end are usually named in the document itself.

- General Power of Attorney assigns the comprehensive right to act on your behalf in a much wider range of circumstances, but ends if you are incapacitated, upon your death, or if you rescind it.
- Durable Power of Attorney, whether general or limited in scope, remains in effect if you are incapacitated.
- Springing Power of Attorney assigns limited or general powers of attorney to your agent only if you are incapacitated.

If you want one person to make healthcare decisions and another to manage your financial concerns, set up limited Springing Powers of Attorney assigning different responsibilities to each agent. As with a living will, review your documents regularly and update them in the event of major life changes, such as marriage or divorce.

"Tax planning is one element of estate planning, and in many estates is the least important factor. The larger issue is: Who will inherit and what will they inherit?"

First National Trust Update April 2015

Estate Planning for Your Legacy

"If I put most of my assets in a Family Limited Partnership, have a buy-out clause covered by life insurance for my practice, and put everything in trust or sign it over to my family in my retirement, can I avoid estate taxes? Do I still need to make a will if everything of value is already dealt with?"

While a large part of estate planning minimizing the tax liability upon death, it's more about ensuring that ownership and control of assets pass to the right person. It's easy to make sure your home, practice, and investments go where you want them to, but don't overlook the smaller items. Family feuds are just as likely over items of sentimental value.

What Is Estate Tax?

Estate tax applies at a federal and ofien state level and is imposed when your possessions and savings are passed on through your will or trusts. The tax comes out of the estate and the beneficiaries don't pay anything themselves.

- Estate tax is calculated on the fair market value of everything you own or in which you have a proprietary interest at time of death, excluding proceeds from life insurance policies and certain types of trust funds.

- Once your Gross Estate is calculated, deductions for mortgages and debts; property passing to surviving spouses and charities; some business operating expenses; and estate administration expenses are allowed.

- The value of lifetime taxable gifis since 1977 are then added to the net amount to calculate the tax due. The tax is then reduced by any available unified credit (your lifetime gifi tax exemption, minus the value of gifis you gave and claimed deductions for while you were alive).

At the federal level, you only must worry about the tax if your estate is worth more than $5,490,000 in 2017. Estate tax at a state level varies according to the state, so be sure to check out the rules for your location.

Why Can't I Just Give It All Away While I'm Alive?

It's tempting to think you avoid estate taxes by giving everything away during your lifetime, but if you aren't careful your estate can get a larger tax bill instead.

That's because your lifetime applicable exclusion for gifis is $5,490,000 in 2017 – the amount at which estate tax becomes due. While you can claim deductions against that of up to $14,000 per donee per year[30], those deductions (previously applied unified credit) are taken from your lifetime credit, reducing the value of the estate you can leave tax-free at the time of death. It's worth noting, however, that you can make unlimited payments directly to medical or educational institutions one someone else's behalf without incurring gifi tax.[31]

Let's take an example to clarify matters. Say at the time of death your estate is worth $10 million. You leave your home and other assets worth $3 million to your spouse and have other deductible expenses of $2 million. Your net estate is then worth $5 million and therefore not subject to estate tax. If you gave away gifis of more than $1.5 million and claimed gifi tax exclusions on them, it's added back to your estate value. Your estate is now $6.5 million, and it becomes liable to tax at 40% on $1.01 million.

If you plan to give away large assets and give items with a fair market value of more than $14,000 to one person in one year, you are liable to gifi tax on the excess value. If

---

[30]Irs.gov,. 2016. "What's New - Estate And Gifi Tax".
https:/ www.irs.gov/Businesses/Small-Businesses-&-Self-E mployed/Whats-New-Estate-and-Gifi-Tax.

[31]Spiegelman, Rande. 2016. "The Estate Tax And Lifetime Gifiing". *Schwab.Com.*
http:/ www.schwab.com/public/schwab/nn/articles/The-Es tate-Tax-and-Lifetime-Gifiing.

you die leaving an estate that doesn't trigger the estate tax, you are probably better off leaving the assets in your estate and including them in your will.

As you can see, the decision to gifi assets during your lifetime vs. upon your death affects the amount of tax you pay and the amount for which your estate is liable, so make large gifis with caution and only afier taking legal advice on their implications both now and later.

In the end, your choice has more to do with when you want your beneficiaries to benefit. If you think it's more important to ensure your children are taken care of later in life, or you want to ensure an inheritance for your grandkids, put money and assets in trust for them. If you're more concerned with helping them out now, use the annual gifi tax exclusions instead.

Can't I Avoid Estate Tax by Setting up a Trust?

You can use trusts to manage your assets both during your lifetime and afier your death. A trust you set up during your life is a Living Trust, whereas one created in your will is a Testamentary Trust. A testamentary trust is irrevocable by nature, but a living trust can be either revocable or irrevocable. You can make amendments to a revocable trust, including removing assets from it during your lifetime. It becomes irrevocable at the time of your death. If you place assets into an irrevocable trust during your lifetime, however, all control over them passes to the trustee and both you and they must follow the trust rules.

Placing assets in an irrevocable trust may remove them from your estate, but they are liable to gifi tax at the time of transfer and the trust is a legal entity requiring an Employer Identification Number (EIN). It has its own costs and must file its own tax return. As such, setting up a trust shouldn't be motivated by tax considerations.

The real advantage of a trust is that it allows you to pass your assets to your beneficiaries without them going through probate upon your death. All assets owned solely by you are frozen until an Estate Executor is appointed. If you are the sole owner of your practice and want to pass it on to a partner or family member without having the business' assets frozen or having the practice wound up, consider setting up a revocable trust and holding your business in it.

Assets in a marital trust are exempt from estate tax, but since assets left to a surviving spouse are exempt anyway the benefit still comes from the ability to avoid probate, rather than to avoid tax.

Do I Really Need to Make a Will?

Yes.

Unless you understand the state's intestacy and community property laws[32] and they happen to mirror your wishes, draw up a will and revise it regularly. Even if you want to distribute your assets, say leaving your practice to one child, your home to another, and your real estate business to a third, you must specify who gets what in your will. If they each inherit one-third and can't agree on an equitable split, most of your estate can well be lost in legal fees.

Perhaps even more important to avoid family squabbles is to include smaller items in your will. If you have promised your wine cellar to someone, document it. Family heirlooms are one of the biggest causes of conflict at what is already a stressful time for all involved.

In addition to naming an executor in your will, if you have young children or elderly parents, name a guardian. You

---

[32] Statutes.legis.state.tx.us,. 2016. "ESTATES CODE CHAPTER 201. DESCENT AND DISTRIBUTION".
http:/ www.statutes.legis.state.tx.us/Docs/ES/htm/ES.201.htm.

might want one person in charge of healthcare or other welfare issues and someone else responsible for financial management.

When you make a will, you will usually do so in front of two witnesses and sign a legally binding written document. Although it is possible to make a will without legal guidance, it's not advisable if you intend to leave a legacy of any size.

Where Can I Get Help with Estate Planning?

When you plan your estate put time and thought into who and what really matters to you. It is always helpful to discuss your estate with loved ones who can help guide you through the daunting task. Independent attorneys are also of immense value and can help you get to grips with the legal aspects of your estate.

Ultimately, it is you who makes the decisions about your property and an attorney can help you come to grips with the formalities and legalities. These are very tough questions, even for professionals.

You can find more detailed information and links to recommended experts on the FinancialWellnessMD.com website.

"It's not how much money you make, but how much money you keep, how hard it works for you, and how many generations you keep it for

- Robert Kiyosaki

Wealth Management and Family Offices

David Drake
Author, *LIFEE Life Instructions for Entrepreneurs and Executives*, Founder and Chairman, LDJ Capital, a family office Tech | Media | Energy | Real Estate
thesoholoft.com/

"I have all these investments and assets, and although I'm pretty good at evaluating an individual investment and building a balanced portfolio, sometimes I feel overwhelmed trying to see where everything fits into the overall strategy. I've heard about family offices and I like the idea of hiring someone to stay on top of everything for me. What do I look for and what do I avoid? Where do the ultra-wealthy put their money?"

In recent years, the world has witnessed the rise of affluent individuals at an unprecedented rate. According to the Capgemini Wealth Management report, the combined wealth of Ultra-High Net Worth Individuals (UHNWIs) in the world stands at approximately 14.7 trillion.

According to James Hughes, lawyer and expert on wealth management, about 85% of the wealth created by rich families is lost by the third generation. In 90% of the cases considered, it was attributed to a lack of proper communication between generations and an inability to make well-informed decisions, especially by the younger generations.

Family offices exist to ensure families retain their wealth across generations. With their roots in Europe and until the 19th century relatively rare, most were ofien connected to French, British and German nobility. Family offices spread during the Industrial Revolution, an era that created great wealth for many innovators of the time. It was the Rockefellers, one of the most well-known ultra-wealthy families, who set up one of the first family offices in the U.S.

It's not surprising that the last decade witnessed a phenomenal rise in family offices, owing largely to the need for best practices in wealth management and preservation in the afiermath of the global financial crisis. Presently, there are about 3000 single family and 150 multi-family offices in the U.S. alone, holding an estimated $1.2 trillion and $450 billion in investments respectively.

Types of Family Offices

The original family offices were non-bank, single-family "boutiques," but as more individuals and families increased their net worth and needed wealth managers, multi-family offices appeared, and private banks also offered competing services.

Single-Family Offices

Single-family offices typically cater to top UHNWIs, those with family wealth of $100 million or more. Originally, their focus was finding suitable investments to manage their clients' wealth. In a bid to secure a larger clientele and better deals, they now provide more personalized services.

Services like helping clients plan travel, employing historians and psychologists for professional assistance are commonplace. A family office is structured to the specific needs of a family business, whether in investing, estate planning, accounting, philanthropy, or even household staffing.

Multi-Family Offices

Many of these UHNWIs with a net worth more than $30 million, but less than $100 million were disqualified from participating in family offices, but nonetheless have a distinct need for their services. The creation and proliferation of multi-family offices allow these wealthy individuals and families to avail themselves of services otherwise beyond their reach.

Since most family offices do not possess large capital bases like their private bank counterparts, the offering of more specialized services comes with high fees. It increases their operational cost and leads to lower profits. To overcome this, some family offices adopted a strategy of charging a fixed annualized fee to clients to cover some operational costs, while outsourcing investments to private banks.

Wealth Management Firms

The number of people with investment-worthy assets worth at least $1 million (excluding primary residence and any collectibles) grew by more than 9%, to touch 12 in 2012, says a report from Capgemini and RBC Wealth

Management. The number of millionaires in North America (the region recording the maximum growth) grew by 11.5% reaching 3.73 million.

Wealth Management Firms have developed to meet the needs of these High Net Worth Individuals (HNWIs) who are not eligible to participate in family offices but still need comprehensive financial management services.

Private Banks

As the number of ultra-high net-worth individuals (UHNWIs) increases globally, more private banks are morphing into big family offices to meet the growing demand for wealth management by affluent families. Today, many large private banks with global reach now have units specially created to offer family office services to the ultra-wealthy.

In addition to wealth management services, these offer other professional services that meet the needs of their clients, from banking, tax advisory, and philanthropic use of their wealth. The banks falter, however, when it comes to offering personalized services to clients.

Private Banks vs Small Non-Bank Boutique Family Offices

The dilemma of the wealthy becomes a choice of the best family office service provider. With so many firms offering similar services it is more difficult to locate those that best suits the needs of a family. In response to this, certain family offices take advantage of the situation by charging families to search through their platform for the best service providers.

In determining which family office provider is the best for your family, look for those that offer services to meet its unique needs. If a family wants help with all its financial and investment needs, a private bank is preferred to a single or multi-family office. If, on the other hand, your family makes its investment decisions privately and only requires an office that offers personalized services such as financial education and professional advice, traditional family offices might serve your needs better. In addition, the years of industry experience of a family office provider are an important factor when making a choice among different alternatives.

The fees charged by family offices are an integral factor to consider. Most family offices charge a fixed fee known as "assets under advisement" fees for the assets they directly control on behalf of their clients. In addition, while there are some that charge hourly rates, others receive fees on an annualized basis for special services offered to clients.

How the Wealthy Allocate Their Assets

Traditionally, a large percentage of family wealth is held in equities. Afier the global financial crisis exposed the high volatility of this investment class, many family offices are diversifying and reallocating their client's investments to less volatile asset classes in a bid to mitigate risk. According to Carmot Capital, an investment management firm, a traditional allocation of assets could have 60% in global equities, 30% in global bonds and 10% invested in alternative asset classes such as real estate. Alternative asset classes, such as real estate, are gaining in popularity.

Real estate presents one of the best alternative asset classes in which to invest, as it provides an opportunity for direct investments with higher yields with minimal risk over the long term. It is a tangible asset that helps investors diversify their portfolios with more consistent cash flows and greater control of returns because it is shielded from market volatility in prices, unlike equities and bonds.

Family offices across the globe, in a bid to diversify their clients' investment portfolios, are already directing large percentages of their assets into real estate as an alternative investment class. According to a report by FOX Investment, the average family office typically invests $46 million in real estate, which represents 12% of its total investments. Set this against the 10% traditionally allocated to all alternative asset classes and it becomes clear real estate is set to become an ever more crucial part of wealth management for UHNWIs and their families.

Leveraging Real Estate Crowdfunding

Family offices are signifying their interest in investing in real estate via crowdfunding deals. Crowdfunding entails gathering small amounts of money from many people. Institutional capital was introduced into real estate crowd funding, with a pioneering move by investment banking firm The Carlton Group, launching its real estate platform. Many family offices also demonstrate their interest in doing the same, encouraged that all real estate deals have been successful.

Private Equity

While private equity has taken a major hit over the past decade, it still represents a large part of a family office's portfolio. Geographically, family offices are reallocating their private equity investments from emerging economies (such as Asian and South American countries) to developed nations, with the U.S., Europe and Japan cited as preferred destinations. Reasons for this move include low returns on investment, the effect of the US government tapering policy, and on falling commodity exports in emerging economies.

Since the SEC passed Title III of the JOBS Act in 2015, online real estate investment was somewhat simplified and made accessible to a wider range of investors through crowdfunding and syndication platforms.

To learn more about crowdfunding and property investment syndication, and how you can become an accredited investor to take advantage of them, visit FinancialwellnessMD.com

Amir Says

Thank you, Drake, for introducing us to family offices and the types of services they offer. For me, the key takeaways are that some of the wealthiest families in the world are consistently moving their investments from equities to real estate and taking advantage of online real estate platforms such as FinancialwellnessMD.com, which allow accredited investors to streamline the investment process.

The other important thing to note is to investigate the fee structures of any financial services company and weigh the costs and advantages carefully before signing on to anything.

Part 4: Take Action

"Vision without action is merely a dream. Action without vision just passes the time. Vision with action can change the world."

Joel A. Barker

What Now?

We've come to the end of our primer on wealth preservation, so now it's time to think about putting all of this together into a simple checklist. You might recognize this as a summary of the key points of the chapters in this book. In fact, you might want to print it out and keep it somewhere you are reminded on a regular basis what you are doing and why.

You can find a printable version of this list at FinancialWellnessMD.com in Book Resources.

Wealth Preservation Checklist

Know Your Why

If you don't know what you want to achieve financially, it's a lot harder to set goals and stay focused. Even more important is knowing why. Are you only interested in saving for a comfortable retirement, or do you want to leave a legacy for your family? Do you have philanthropic goals?

Commit to Learning

If your medical training hasn't prepared you for financial success, but it's important to you, accept that there will be a learning curve, and commit to your financial education.

Enjoy the Journey

While it's important to have goals and work towards them, you don't want to be so focused on the future that you forget to enjoy the present. Recognize and celebrate every achievement along the way.

Stay Positive

Setbacks happen. Failure is only permanent if you chose not to learn from it. Never be afraid to ask questions and make decisions.

Learn to Budget

At every stage of your financial journey, knowing what you have, what you're earning and what you're spending is essential. A realistic budget will keep you on track, but you must work within it for it to be effective.

Tackle Your Debts

Pay off crippling bad debts to make sure you are not a slave to compound interest. Understand the difference between bad debt, which keeps you starved of resources, and good debt, which allows you to make the most of your money.

Budget Your Business

Apply the same money-management principles to your personal and business finances. Have a plan, stick to it, and know when to cash out.

Build Your Buffer

Once you've tackled your debts, build a cash buffer to inoculate you against short-term cash flow crises. Never invest money long-term you need access to at short notice. Get life and own-occupation disability insurance.

Understand Income Types

Know the three types of income:

- Active income, where you trade hours for dollars
- Portfolio Income, where you make capital gains on the sale of assets
- Passive income, where assets you own earn money for you

Focus on portfolio and passive income if you want to build your net worth.

Know Your Investor Style

Are you an active or passive investor? What is your attitude to risk? Create a long-term investment strategy to reach your goals in a way that works for you.

Follow Your Plan

Don't be swayed by market conditions and pundits' opinions. Base your decisions on your own goals, and on your own portfolio's performance.

Look Beyond Headline Figures

Always question the source of figures, and how they are calculated. Remember to factor in associated fees.

Be Prepared to Walk Away

There will never be a shortage of opportunities. If the numbers don't stack up, or you can't get a straight answer to your questions, don't let fear of missing out force your hand. The deal of the decade occurs more ofien than you think.

Leverage Your Investment with Real Estate

Understand how leverage works to maximize the return on your investment. Remember, real estate provides important collateral and insurability of leveraged debt unavailable in most other asset classes.

Understand Risks

Learn the difference between alpha risk (past performance) beta risk (volatility) and gamma (asset control.) Only compare like with like when considering the risks of multiple investment options, to avoid confusion.

Keep Your Eye on the Ball

There's a difference between a long-term investment strategy and failing to adjust your portfolio based on its performance. Review your assets periodically, and make sure they are still a good fit.

Get to grips with Taxes

Reduce your tax liability by making the most of tax deductions, setting up an LLC, and using tax-efficient investment vehicles.

Understand Pensions

Learn the difference between Traditional and Roth pension plans and work out whether you would be better paying taxes now or deferring them until retirement. Consider setting up a self-directed IRA to take advantage of a wider range of asset classes and increasing your control over your pension fund's growth.

Make Sure You're Covered

Consider the different types of insurance. At a minimum, make sure you have your own occupation disability insurance, and a permanent life insurance policy. If you need additional cover for key personnel, to pay off a mortgage, or to provide additional funds in specific circumstances, consider term insurance for those.

Put It in Trust, or Limit Liability

Protect personal assets from business failures and protect family members and business partners from one member's poor decisions by holding assets in trusts or limited liability business entities, such as LLCs and Family Limited Partnerships.

Use Financial Arbitrage

Once you've built up a healthy cash value in your permanent life insurance policy, use it to take advantage of low-interest loans and invest the money in higher-yield investments.

Beware the Posse

As your net worth grows, you will be exposed to investment opportunities previously unavailable to you. You will also attract the attention of scammers, con-artists, and hangers-on. Learn to spot the signs of a bad deal and trust your own instincts. Stick to your plan.

Make the Most of Charity

Giving is good for your health, makes you happy, and creates community ties. If you're donating money, know what you can deduct from your tax return to make the most of your donations.

Plan for Your Later Years

Use a living will and powers of attorney to ensure you'll be taken care of the way you want to be in your later years.

Plan for Your Legacy

No one likes to think about death but make a will to ensure your assets are distributed how you want them to be once you're gone. Use trusts and life insurance to avoid probate and ensure your estate will have sufficient cash to pay estate taxes.

Consider Future Generations

If you want to ensure your grandchildren and their grandchildren are taken care of, consider the services of a family office, to prevent one generation's poor decisions wiping out your family's wealth.

If you keep all these points in mind, you won't go far wrong. Of course, that doesn't mean every investment is guaranteed to generate the returns you expect, or that you won't have the occasional loss. But one poor decision shouldn't wipe you out or prevent you reaching your goals.

If you want to take the next steps in your financial education, join us at FinancialWellnessMD.com in the Book Resources section, where many of the topics covered here are explored in more detail.

If you're interested in real estate investment opportunities I have a special invitation for you in the next chapter.

"Diversification is a protection against ignorance. It makes very little sense for those who know what they're doing"

-**Warren Buffett**

Join Me at Financial Wellness MD

I mentioned in the preface to this book – and a few times throughout – that in addition to being a board-certified Anesthesiologist, I have Series 63 and 22 securities licenses and run my own real estate investment business. I make no attempt to hide my personal preferences when it comes to investment strategies. For me, real estate is where it's at.

According to Fortune Builders, 77% of American millionaires chose real estate as their primary investment vehicle in 2014.[33] That's because unlike other investments, a well-managed real estate portfolio can provide long-term protection for your wealth, while also securing your retirement and financial goals.

What headlines like these don't tell you, though, is that most of this in in commercial, industrial, or institutional real estate – the kinds of deals that most investors were prevented from taking advantage of due to high barriers to

---

[33] FortuneBuilders,. 2014. "8 Out Of 10 Millionaires Choose Real Estate Investing For 2014". http:/ www.fortunebuilders.com/8-10-millionaires-choose-real-estate-investing-2014/.

Vice President's Report	Dr. [illegible]	
Secretary's Report	Dr. Meher Medavaram	2 min
Treasurer's Budget (Action Item)	Dr. Sumul Raval	10 min
Past President Report	Dr. Anupama Gotimukula	2 min
BOT Chair Report	Dr. V. Ranga	2 min
YPS President Reports	Dr. Pooja Kinkhabwala	2 min
MSRF President Report	Dr. Ammu Susheela	2 min
Regional Directors Reports	12 x 1 min	12 min
Update on AAPI 2022 Convention	Dr. Jayesh Shah	3 min
AAPI Charitable Foundation Report	Dr. Ajeet Singhvi	3 min
Committee Chairs Reports	11 x 1 min	11 min
Old Business		5 min
New Business		5 min
Adjourn		11.30 am

AAPI ANNUAL GOVERNING BODY – 2022
SAN ANTONIO, TX
Sunday, June 26 2022

Governing Body Meeting – 9.30 am to 11.30 am CST

AGENDA

9.30 am
Welcome & Opening Remarks
& appointment of speaker   Dr. Ravi Kolli
Call to Order   (Speaker)
Establish Quorum   Dr. Meher Medavaram
Introductions of the members

| President's Report | Dr. Ravi Kolli | 5 min |

DRAFT

entry in the past. In fact, most investors were never even aware of these deals, as they are negotiated privately and snapped up by the wealthiest investors before anyone else even heard about them.

It's only in recent years, with the advent of crowd funding, these investments opened to smaller investors. I started sending out emails about investment and real estate in September 2015 to close friends and colleagues. As the emails became more popular, it made sense to set up a website where subscribers and readers could join me to learn more.

FinancialWellnessMD.com aims to provide you with a financial and investment education. You'll find links to tools and resources, downloadable reports, eBooks and other content to help you take the first few steps in your investment journey, and the podcast and blog, all in one place.

Join me at FinancialWellnessMD.com today to find out more and take the first steps to building your real estate and investment portfolio.

References

Made in the USA
Coppell, TX
21 June 2022